Women Priests
in the Episcopal Church

The Experience of the First Decade

by
Mary S. Donovan

Forward Movement Publications, Cincinnati, Ohio

1831965

BX
5965
·D65
1988

Photo: Elizabeth Gomes

Mary Sudman Donovan (Ph. D., Columbia) is lecturer in history at the University of Arkansas at Little Rock, where she makes her home with her husband, Herbert, bishop of Arkansas. Her writings include *A Different Call: Women's Ministries in the Episcopal Church, 1850-1920,* published by Morehouse-Barlow.

Cover: The Rev. Fran Toy

©1988. *Forward Movement Publications,* 412 Sycamore Street, Cincinnati, Ohio 45202-4195. Printed in U.S.A.

Preface

To assess the effect of women priests upon the Episcopal Church, I have interviewed women and men throughout the United States. This book is shaped by their testimony. In this venture, I have been amazed and encouraged by the openness with which people have been willing to share their own faith journeys, an openness that testifies to the deep affection in which so many women priests are held. I am profoundly grateful to all those people who answered my inquiries with such diligence and care.

My particular gratitude goes to the women priests who agreed to be featured in this volume. I have depended upon each of them for extensive assistance. We have talked and written and exchanged ideas and comments. I know there have been moments when many of them wondered why they ever agreed to take part in this project! But as we worked, I developed a great admiration for their spiritual leadership and personal dedication. Their willingness to share their own personal stories at the risk of public exposure and criticism indicates the depth of their commitment to ordination of women as priests. From them, I learned more than I can ever say.

To select the clergywomen who appear here, I wrote to bishops, priests and laity in many parts of the country asking them to suggest candidates. From that initial list, the featured priests were selected to demonstrate the wide variety of ministries that today's clergywomen exercise. Although in my opinion, each of these women is an outstanding priest, she is like hundreds of her sister priests whose stories are yet to be told. I've presented these particular portraits simply to add personality to an abstract issue— to help us grasp the immense ramifications of opening the priest-hood to women.

So many other people have had a part in this work. Presiding Bishop Edmond L. Browning was a steady source of encourage-ment. Sandra Boyd and Suzanne Hiatt gave me access to the data on clergywomen which they have so carefully assembled. Polly and Christoph Keller and David E. Sumner shared their files on

96 0205

ordination of women with me. Fredrica H. Thompsett and the Episcopal Divinity School arranged a place for me to live and work for one semester. Elinor S. Hearne and V. Nelle Bellamy provided answers and information from the Archives of the Episcopal Church. Elizabeth Jay, Diana Morris, David L. Seger, Ann Smith and Alexander D. Stewart gave me special assistance from their various departments at the Episcopal Church Center; and Beth Matthews was a ready source of information from the Diocese of Arkansas. Charles H. Long at Forward Movement believed in the project and Robert Horine helped to shape it. Fred Darragh and several anonymous donors provided financial assistance. And my husband, Herbert, was an invaluable copyreader, confidant and cheerleader all along the way.

Mary S. Donovan
February 4, 1988
Little Rock, Arkansas

The 1976 Convention

The gallery of the Minneapolis Convention Center was filled to overflowing on the afternoon of September 16, 1976. The House of Deputies was in session. It was an extraordinary occasion and the usual onlookers—friends and relatives of deputies, local church members, young churchmen, office staff members—had been joined by most of the church's bishops, men and women from all of the church's seminaries, official representatives from a host of Episcopal organizations, and reporters from both the religious and the secular press. The deputies were about to vote on the ordination of women as priests and bishops.

The Very Reverend David Collins, chairman of the Committee on Ministry, moved concurrence with the House of Bishops, which had already passed the amendment to the canons: "The provisions of these canons for the admission of Candidates, and for the Ordination to the three Orders, Bishops, Priests, and Deacons, shall be equally applicable to men and women." The debate which followed was heated, yet orderly. Speeches, limited to two minutes, alternated between affirmative and negative positions. A total of fifty-eight deputies spoke. Then, Collins announced, "The last five minutes of our report will be silence. We need to pray for guidance in our vote. We need to pray even more for that time afterward when the results are announced. I plead that there will be no winners and no losers."

People rose to their feet and bowed their heads. As the emotional pressure built, hands reached out from one spectator to the next, seeking both connection and support—sometimes from friends, sometimes from strangers. "I don't believe I have ever stood in the midst of such an electrical silence," Deacon Peggy Bosmyer remembered.

At the end of five minutes, the Reverend John B. Coburn, president of the House of Deputies, called for the vote. Diocesan delegations polled their members, marked their ballots and handed them to the tellers. Minor business was enacted during what seemed an interminable wait. Then the tellers returned; attention

3

focused on the podium. Quickly, Coburn announced the vote. The resolution had passed in both orders. The vote in the clerical order was 60 affirmative, 39 negative, 15 divided; in the lay order it was 64 affirmative, 36 negative and 13 divided. There was a scattering of applause, but chiefly there was silence, as if each hearer were taking a moment to internalize the news, to rethink the decision in his or her own mind, and to comprehend the magnitude of the change that had just occurred.

With the reading of three prayers by the House chaplain, the Reverend Dr. Massey Shepherd, the session adjourned. Then the reaction burst forth—hugs and cheers and joy in the faces of those who had supported the resolution, anger and tears and silence from those who opposed it. The vote just announced had shaken the Episcopal Church to its very foundation.

This book is being written eleven years after that historic event. It is an update on the status of women priests in the Episcopal Church and a review of the effect of their ministries on their church. By focusing upon particular women priests and charting their spiritual journeys, the book translates the abstract issues into personal stories of the people of God. The most faithful way to judge the effect on the Episcopal Church of ordination of women to priesthood is through the compounding of hundreds of individual interactions in parishes and missions and diocesan programs throughout this province of the Anglican Communion.

Women in the Episcopal Church

The call to ministry was not new to Episcopal women; throughout the church's history women had responded to that call in various ways. Women were the work force of most local parishes. They taught the children, cleaned the church, prepared the altar and were the mainstays of innumerable fund-raising campaigns. Some women invested their time and talents in the church's organizations. Others worked as parish secretaries, directors of Christian education, or administrators of church sponsored institutions. Some were missionaries, teaching and healing, ministering to those in need in domestic and foreign missionary posts. Making a lifetime commitment, a few women joined Episcopal sisterhoods

4

or became deaconesses, pledging their lives to service to others.[1]

Although in their inmost thoughts some of these women may have considered the possibility of priesthood, the great majority made no public statements suggesting such a possibility. English women, as early as 1909, had organized the Church League for Women's Suffrage and some of the more radical members of the group, like Maude Royden, added ordination of women to the priesthood to their demands for political representation.[2] But in the United States there was no widespread public agitation for women's ordination prior to the 1960s.

The political structure of the Episcopal Church, as it had developed over two centuries, excluded women not only from the priesthood but from participation in many phases of the political life of the church. As late as the 1960s the church, by tradition and legislation, was effectively divided into two spheres—one for women and one for men. Within the local parish men and women worshiped together, but most other activities were segregated by gender. Women's activities centered in such organizations as the Episcopal Church Women, the altar guild, the Daughters of the King, or the Girls' Friendly Society. Though some parishes had men's clubs or chapters of the Brotherhood of St. Andrew, most men found their primary involvement with the church in serving as ushers and members of the vestry. In almost half the dioceses, only men could serve on vestries or as deputies to diocesan conventions. Nationally, no women could serve as deputies to General Convention.[3]

As the feminist movement gained strength in the early 1960s, women began to examine their lives and to set personal goals. But as they worked toward those aims, they often found themselves thwarted, locked into gender roles dictated by culture, tradition and law. Faced with this situation, many feminists decided to challenge the barriers.

Growing interest in ordination

In the case of the Episcopal Church, sexual segregation had scarcely been named, let alone challenged, before 1970. The fact that a majority of church members were barred from serving as deputies to the church's supreme governing assembly raised little or no concern in the hearts of most Episcopalians. Toward the end of the decade, though, the growing national feminist consciousness began to subject ecclesiastical practices to the same scrutiny used for other aspects of society, questioning whether the Christian gospel was meant to apply differently to women than to men. That question surfaced in a variety of settings—informal discussions in ECW meetings, seminary classrooms, gatherings of professional women church workers. Quietly at first, then with growing voice, women began to ask, "Why does the Episcopal Church refuse to ordain women to the priesthood?" More and more women attended seminaries and many, finding themselves perfectly able to do seminary work, asked why they should be barred from priesthood.[4]

The 1967 and 1970 conventions

Several important General Convention decisions set the stage for consideration of ordination of women to priesthood. In 1967, the convention voted to amend the church's constitution to enable women to serve as deputies to the national convention. That vote was ratified at the 1970 convention in Houston and several female deputies were seated. Representatives there also voted to admit women to the diaconate and granted women serving as deaconesses the same status as male deacons.

The 1970 convention was also the first to consider the possibility of ordaining women to priesthood. A general resolution affirming that "women are eligible to seek and accept ordering to the diaconate and to the priesthood and to be ordained and consecrated to the episcopate" was introduced and debated extensively. When finally put to a vote, the resolution was narrowly defeated. The vote was clerical: 38¼ yes, 31¾ no, 21 divided; lay: 49¼ yes, 28¾ no, 13 divided. (Divided votes had the effect of negative votes according to House of Deputies rules of order.) Meeting concurrently, the Episcopal Church Women approved a similar recommendation by a vote of 222 to 45.[5]

The 1973 convention

At the 1973 General Convention in Louisville the issue of ordination of women to priesthood was again introduced. Proponents felt, because of the close vote in Houston, that passage was likely. However, in the intervening three years the opposition had organized and the furor over revising *The Book of Common Prayer* had produced a conservative swing in election of deputies in many dioceses. The resolution that the Episcopal Church "provide for the ordination of women" by rewriting the canons on ordination to state that they "shall be equally applicable to men and women" was debated vigorously. When the vote was taken, the resolution was defeated. The vote was clerical: 50 yes, 43 no, 20 divided; lay: 49 yes, 37 no, 26 divided. Although a majority of individuals in the House had voted yes, the divided votes by diocesan deputations added to the negative votes killed the resolution.[6]

The defeat was a stunning blow to proponents of the measure. In the attempt to analyze the reasons for the defeat, those who favored priesthood for women gradually divided into two camps. One group felt there had been weaknesses in the political strategy at Louisville—leadership too concentrated in the northeastern dioceses, not enough effort to develop a broad geographical basis, the need to develop and strengthen alliances with other church organizations, particularly the ECW. A more sophisticated effort to correct those weaknesses would produce an affirmative vote at the next convention. The other group came to the conclusion that "the democratic process, the political dynamics, and the legal guidelines" were "out of step with the divine imperative which says, now is the time."[7] The latter group began to explore the possibility of ordaining women without General Convention action.

The Philadelphia ordinations

On the feast of St. Mary and St. Martha, July 29, 1974, eleven women deacons were ordained to the priesthood in the Church of the Advocate in Philadelphia. "We are certain that the church needs women in priesthood to be true to the gospel understanding of human unity in Christ," explained the eleven ordinands in a public statement. "Our primary motivation is to begin to free priesthood from the bondage it suffers as long as it is characterized by categorical exclusion of persons on the basis of sex. We do not feel we are 'hurting the cause,' for the 'cause' is not merely to admit a few token women to the 'privilege' of priesthood. We must rather reaffirm and recover the universality of Christ's ministry as symbolized in that order."[8] Believing that a dramatic act of "obedience to the Spirit" would most clearly present to the church the urgency of the question, three bishops had agreed to be the ordaining bishops.[9]

The Philadelphia ordinations, and a subsequent service in Washington, D.C., on September 7, 1975 in which four other women were ordained priest, focused the church's attention on the ordination issue and attracted widespread national publicity. The House of Bishops, meeting in special session, declared that the "necessary conditions for valid ordination to the priesthood" were not fulfilled in those ordinations and voted to "decry the action" of the bishops who presided in Philadelphia. However, at its regular meeting later that fall, the House of Bishops reiterated its support "in principle" for the ordination of women to priesthood by a vote of 97 to 35 with 6 abstentions.[10]

Ordination approved

Thus the stage was set for the meeting of the General Convention in 1976. Groups favoring and opposing ordination had worked to elect deputies representing their points of view. Many churchwomen had internalized women's ordination as an issue that affected their own position within the ecclesiastical structure. Bishops across the country had been confronted with their roles as guardians of "the faith, unity, and discipline of the church." Men priests were faced with the question of whether their gender was a necessary qualification for ordination. All these factors combined to produce a favorable decision.

On September 15, the House of Bishops voted 95 to 61, with 2 abstentions, to amend the canons to provide that women as well as men were eligible for ordination as bishops, priests or deacons. The next day the House of Deputies also approved and the change took effect on January 1, 1977. The House of Bishops also provided that each woman who had been ordained before 1977 could function as a priest after a "completion of the ritual acts performed" in Philadelphia or Washington. A public event was called for in which each woman was to appear with her bishop, but the nature of the event was not specified, except for the acknowledgment that it was not to be a "reordination." With the exception of Marie Moorefield, who had left the Episcopal Church to become a Methodist in 1975, all the previously ordained women went through such services in 1977.[11]

Ordinations were held throughout the United States in the early months of 1977 as women who had served as deacons for varying numbers of years came forward to be ordained priest. By the end of the year, about one hundred women had been ordained priest. Since many of these women had been working toward ordination for several years, the large majority of them were already employed in ecclesiastical positions. They worked in parishes and missions, as chaplains in schools and hospitals and in a variety of diocesan jobs.[12]

The change in the church's official position also opened the door to women who had been hesitant to apply for candidacy until a decision about priesthood for women had been reached. Commissions on ministry in one diocese after another began to consider female as well as male candidates. The number of women at Episcopal seminaries grew. In 1977, there were women in the M. Div. programs at each of the church's seminaries (163 women total); by 1987, women made up thirty-nine per cent of the M. Div. candidates at Episcopal seminaries.[13]

Forces of division

Support for ordination of women, however, was by no means unanimous and some Episcopalians continued their opposition even after the 1976 decision. Immediately after the General Convention, the Fellowship of Concerned Churchmen, a coalition of organizations opposing ordination of women, announced its

9

intention to consider an alternative ecclesiastical organization, declaring that the Episcopal Church had "no right or authority to change the nature of the Apostolic priesthood and episcopate." It invited all Episcopalians dissatisfied with the General Convention's actions to gather the following September in St. Louis. Though ordination of women was one of the primary points of dissatisfaction, prayer book revision, the ordination of homosexuals and church funding of programs for minority groups were also major areas of concern.[14]

In the ensuing months, a few parishes withdrew from the Episcopal Church and began to form alliances among themselves. Laity and priests from those churches were among the 1,746 registrants at the St. Louis congress in September, 1977. After three days of meeting, the participants decided to form a new church which they tentatively called the Anglican Church of North America. The church's three orders of ministry—bishop, priest and deacon—would be limited to men; women could serve as deaconesses.

The subsequent history of the Anglican Church of North America is too complex to be detailed here. Plagued by internal dissention, the original body has divided into at least five separate churches. However, the number of Episcopalians who transferred allegiances to the dissident churches has been relatively small. In 1985, after a detailed study of Episcopal splinter groups, the Reverend Don S. Armentrout, professor of ecclesiastical history at the School of Theology of the University of the South, listed the total population of all the post-1976 splinter groups at about 15,000 members, less than half of one per cent of the total number of Episcopalians.[15]

House of Bishops, 1977

In the fall of 1977, however, there was still uncertainty about the strength of the secession movement. That uncertainty was very much on the minds of bishops as they gathered for their annual meeting at Port St. Lucie, Florida just two weeks after the St. Louis congress, on September 30, 1977. In his opening address,

Presiding Bishop John Allin highlighted the need to find ways to deal with "divisions and fragmentations in the Church," and then admitted that even he found himself at that point "unable to accept women in the role of priest." Though he offered to resign as Presiding Bishop, the House rejected his offer and affirmed "the right of the Presiding Bishop to hold a personal conviction on this issue."[16]

Much of the remainder of the meeting was focused on reconciliation. The bishops adopted a statement on collegiality that recognized "sharp differences of conscientious conviction" and upheld the need for sensitivity, patience and forbearance "expressed in a willingness to listen, to communicate and to learn." In "An Appeal to Those Who Have Separated Themselves From Our Church," they wrote, "we are certain that it is not necessary for you to leave the Episcopal Church in order to live with your Christian conscience and witness." And finally, they composed a pastoral letter which affirmed "that one is not a disloyal Episcopalian if he or she abstains from supporting the decision (to ordain women) or continues to be convinced it was an error." By the end of the Port St. Lucie meeting, most bishops felt that by accepting an individual's right of conscientious disagreement, the unity of the Episcopal Church would be preserved.[17]

Lambeth Conference, 1978

The following year in its resolution on the ordination of women to the priesthood and the episcopate, the Lambeth Conference took a similar position. Acknowledging that both the debate about ordination of women and the ordinations themselves "have, in some Churches, caused distress and pain to many on both sides," the bishops stated that "To heal these and to maintain and strengthen fellowship is a primary pastoral responsibility of all, and especially of the bishops." Noting that the diocese of Hong Kong, the Anglican Church of Canada, the Episcopal Church in the United States of America, and the Church of the Province of New Zealand had all "admitted women to the presbyterate," the bishops urged those churches to "respect the convictions of those

Provinces and dioceses that do not" and vice versa. The resolution went on to urge that the Anglican Consultative Council both explore "ways in which the fullest use can be made of women's gifts within the total ministry of the Church" and "maintain, and wherever possible extend, the present dialogue with Churches outside the Anglican family."[18]

With the Port St. Lucie resolution, reinforced by the general tone of the Lambeth statement, declaring toleration for those Episcopalians who could not conscientiously accept the ordination of women, the Episcopal Church had averted any large scale division. Gradually over the next ten years, ordination of women found acceptance in more and more dioceses. Some opposition bishops retired, to be replaced by bishops who favored women priests. Other bishops changed their positions and came to support ordination of women for a variety of reasons. The extent of the change within the House of Bishops is indicated by a comparison of two votes. In 1976, the vote approving ordination of women had been ninety-five to sixty-one; at the 1987 House of Bishops, the resolution approving the report of the Committee on Women in the Episcopate passed by a vote of 113 to 17. Immediately after the vote, four of those seventeen bishops rose to state that their negative votes did not indicate opposition to ordination of women.[19]

More indicative of broad acceptance by the Episcopal Church, however, is the widespread deployment of women clergy. The following chapter will examine the distribution of clergywomen both in terms of their occupational situations and their geographical locations. These statistics point to a far deeper theological reality. In the words of one woman priest, "Although I find myself disappointed and frustrated at times, I am also somewhat amazed that we're doing so well as we are, considering the magnitude of the change. My guess is that we were only dimly aware of how significantly this development will alter our understanding of God, and that we will become increasingly aware of the theological significance of ordaining women as the church lives with male and female clergy over the next few years."[20]

Footnotes

1. Mary Sudman Donovan, *A Different Call: Women's Ministries in the Episcopal Church, 1850-1920* (Wilton, CT: Morehouse-Barlow, 1986).

2. Brian Heeney, "The Beginnings of Church Feminism: Women and the Councils of the Church of England, 1897-1919," in Gail Malmgreen, ed., *Religion in the Lives of English Women, 1760-1930* (Bloomington: Indiana University Press, 1986), pp. 272-274.

3. Thirty-four (of seventy-seven) dioceses did not allow women to serve on vestries or be deputies to diocesan conventions in 1964. "Women and the Franchise," *The Episcopalian,* April 24, 1964, p. 20.

4. No women were enrolled in B.D. or M. Div. programs in Episcopal seminaries until 1958 when three women entered the Episcopal Theological School in Cambridge, Massachusetts. By 1976, there were 159 women enrolled in such programs at Episcopal seminaries. Board for Theological Education Reports, published in *The Blue Book* prepared for each General Convention.

5. General Convention rules provide that divided votes have the effect of negative votes. When a vote by orders is taken the measure must pass in both the laity and the clerical orders. Because the measure failed in the House of Deputies, it was not considered in the House of Bishops. General Convention, *Journal,* 1970, p. 160. The final tabulation as listed in the 1970 *Journal* is incorrect. The correct totals appear in *The Living Church,* 8 November 1970, p. 10.

6. General Convention, *Journal,* 1973, pp. 222-225.

7. Paul Washington, "Address to the Congregation," Episcopal Church of the Advocate, Philadelphia, July 29, 1974.

8. Merrill Bittner, Alla Bozarth-Campbell, Alison Cheek, Emily Hewitt, Carter Heyward, Suzanne Hiatt, Marie Moorefield, Jeanette Piccard, Betty Schiess, Katrina Swanson, and Nancy Wittig, "An Open Letter," July 20, 1974.

9. Daniel Corrigan, Robert DeWitt, Edward R. Welles II, "An Open Letter," July 24, 1974.

10. Lee McGhee, Alison Palmer, Betty Rosenberg and Diane Tickell were ordained in Washington, D.C. by Bishop George Barrett. General Convention, *Journal,* 1976, pp. A-9, B-255-259, B-311-317, B-326-332.

11. *Book of Common Prayer,* 1979, p. 517; General Convention, *Journal,* 1976, pp. B-54, B-121, 130-134, 146-148, C-5, D-64-68. Heather Ann Huyck, *To Celebrate a Whole Priesthood,* Ph. D. dissertation, University of Minnesota, 1981, p. 201.

Marie Moorefield Fleischer returned to the Episcopal Church and was reinstated as a priest by Bishop Paul Moore of New York in 1985. She serves as vicar of St. Andrew's Church, Clear Springs, Md.

12. For a more complete history of the women's ordination movement, see Suzanne R. Hiatt, "How We Brought the Good News from Graymoor to Minneapolis: An Episcopal Paradigm," *Journal of Ecumenical Studies* 20 (Fall 1983), p. 580; David E. Sumner, *The Episcopal Church's History, 1945-1985* (Wilton, CT: Morehouse-Barlow, 1987), Chapters 1 and 2; Huyck, *To Celebrate;* Shirley Sartori, *Conflict and Institutional Change: The Ordination of Women in the Episcopal Church,* Ph. D. dissertation, State University of New York at Albany, 1978.

13. Board for Theological Education, "Seminary Enrollment Data" from report to General Convention published in *The Blue Book,* 1979, 1987 figures from the Board for Theological Education office at the Episcopal Church Center.

14. Louis E. Traycik, "The Continuing Church Today," *The Christian Challenge,* February, March, April, 1983.

15. Don S. Armentrout, "Episcopal Splinter Groups: Schisms in the Episcopal Church, 1963-1985," *Historical Magazine of the Protestant Episcopal Church,* 55 (1986): 295-320. Five parishes withdrew from the Episcopal Church to associate themselves with the Roman Catholic Church as "Anglican-Use" parishes under a 1980 agreement with the Vatican. The Vatican has also been willing to accept former Episcopal priests, married or celibate, provided that they are ordained again in the Roman Catholic Church. To date, fewer than forty Episcopal priests have made that transition. Joseph H. Fichter, "Parishes for Anglican Usage," *America,* 14 November 1987, pp. 354-357.

16. General Convention, *Journal,* 1979, pp. B-158-160, 203.

17. Ibid., pp. B-204, 221, 225.

18. Nelle Bellamy, "Participation of Women in the Public Life of the Church from Lambeth Conference 1867-1978," A Research Document prepared for ARC-USA, 1981, pp. 15-17.

19. Minutes of the House of Bishops, 1987, p. 23.

20. Martha Horne to Mary Donovan, 30 December 1987.

Current status of clergywomen

✳ Over 1,200 women have been ordained priest or deacon in the Episcopal Church in the United States. The most recent figures available indicate that, as of November 1, 1987, there were 826 women priests and 410 women deacons in the Episcopal Church.[1] Of that total, 59 deacons and 96 priests were ordained in 1987 and hence do not appear in the following comparisons.

According to official diocesan reports as of January 1, 1987, women made up 8 per cent of the total clergy (bishops, priests and deacons) of the domestic dioceses of the Episcopal Church.[2] Six per cent of all U.S. Episcopal priests were women; 31 per cent of all U.S. deacons were women. A large number of these deacons consider themselves permanent deacons (not candidates for priesthood): 209 women (59 per cent of the female deacons) as compared to 553 men (69 per cent of male deacons).

Among the priests, 79 men and 17 women were ordained under the special provisions of Title III, Canon 11 for ministry to "small, isolated, remote" communities or those with distinctive ethnic composition. Thus, U.S. women are serving in all categories of ordained ministry except the episcopate. The chart on page 17 lists the total numbers and percentages of men and women priests and deacons as of the first of January, 1987.

In terms of deployment, 214 women priests (29 per cent of all women priests) are in charge of congregations—as rectors, vicars or interim pastors. Women serve as rectors of a large variety of parishes. Nancy McGrath is the rector of St. Stephen's, a church of over 600 members in Troy, Michigan.[3] In 1984, Sallie E. Shippen became Oregon's first woman rector at Grace Church in Astoria, one of the oldest churches in the diocese. St. Francis of Assisi Church in Chapin, South Carolina, is a mid-sized parish of which Elizabeth W. Libbey serves as rector. Vienna Anderson is rector of St. Margaret's in Washington, D.C., a church of over 400 members. In Houston, Texas, Helen Havens has been rector of St. Stephen's Church, a congregation of over 800 members, since

1981. Glenis Mollegen is rector of a Connecticut parish, St. Paul's Church, Willimantic (300 members).

Many women serve small rural congregations. Sandra Ann Holmberg's ministry stretches across the state line from St. John's, Moorhead, Minnesota, to St. Stephen's in Fargo, North Dakota. Janice Hotze has been vicar at St. Phillips, Wrangell, Alaska, since 1983. Bonnie Clark is vicar of the Church of the Holy Communion in rural South Carolina. Margaret Babcock is vicar of St. John's Mission in Williams, Arizona. Abigail Painter Hamilton is a white woman serving as rector of a predominantly black congregation in Newark, New Jersey, while Nan Peete, a black woman, is rector of All Saints, Indianapolis, a predominantly white parish. Elaine Kebba is rector of St. Mary's Church in the blue-collar community of Haledon, New Jersey.

In more than a hundred families husband and wife are ordained. These couples work out their professional life in a variety of ways. Anne and Allan Weatherholt live in Hancock, Maryland, where he is the rector of St. Thomas Church while she serves as assistant at All Saints' Church in nearby Frederick. In the far northwestern corner of Montana, Bob Honeychurch is in charge of two congregations at Libby and Troy while his wife, Sylvia Sweeney, serves as a youth circuit rider and a counselor at a Family Planning Clinic. Judith and William Boli are co-rectors of an urban Michigan parish. In an agricultural area of California, Bavi and Robert Moore are co-rectors of St. George's, Salinas.

Increasingly, bishops are appointing women priests to serve as interim ministers—priests who take charge of a congregation during a lengthy search procedure or during a time of reassessment or adjustment. Harriet Burton is functioning in this way in the Diocese of Eastern Oregon. Willa Marie Goodfellow serves as interim rector of St. John's Church, Cedar Rapids, Iowa. Using women as interim ministers has proved to be a successful means of introducing congregations to the possibility of having a woman rector. Sarah Chandler became rector of St. Peter's Church, Windsor, Connecticut, after Margaret Hutchins had served there as interim minister.

PAROCHIAL LIST	PRESBYTERS*				DEACONS			
	Male		Female		Male		Female	
IN CHARGE	#	%	#	%	#	%	#	%
Income from congregation	5193	42	194	27	21	3	6	2
Income from secular source	293	2	20	3	33	4	9	3
TOTAL, IN CHARGE	5486	45	214	29	54	7	15	4
ASSISTING								
Income from congregation	877	7	227	31	96	12	77	22
Income from secular source	313	3	57	8	349	45	122	35
TOTAL ASSISTING	1190	10	284	39	445	57	199	57
NON-PAROCHIAL LIST								
Church related employment	1141	9	117	16	43	6	39	11
Secular employment	1432	12	73	10	131	17	41	12
Other employment	399	3	29	4	38	5	31	9
Retired persons	2603	21	13	2	68	9	26	7
TOTAL NON-PAROCHIAL	5575	46	232	32	280	36	137	39
GRAND TOTAL	12251		730		779		351	
NUMBER OF CLERGY								
Canon III.1 Priests	87		22					
Perpetual Deacons					553		209	
Other Deacons					226		142	
TOTAL	12251		730		779		351	

*Bishops are not included in any of these statistics.
SOURCE: Episcopal Church Center, *Compilation of Annual Diocesan Reports, 1986* Figures as of September 4, 1987.

The largest category in which clergywomen serve is that of parish assistant or associate. Of the women priests, 39 per cent serve in these categories as do 57 per cent of the deacons. Assisting roles take many forms. Often women serve as associate rectors as does Robin Moore at St. Mark's Church, Jonesboro, Arkansas, or Sandra Michels at St. Martin's Church, Ellisville, Missouri. Some large churches are beginning to require that their clerical staffs include women and men. There are two women priests— Elizabeth Sherman and Nancy Roth—on the staff of Trinity Church, Wall Street. Judith Baumer has been at St. Bartholomew's, New York City, since 1981. Davette Turk is the assistant at the Church of the Redeemer in Jacksonville, Florida. But this trend is not yet universal. In Atlanta, Georgia, for example, of seven churches with multiple-member clerical staffs, only two include women clergy: Barbara Brown Taylor is at All Saints; Pat Merchant is the only clergywoman among the priests at St. Luke's. Eight per cent of the women priests who are parish assistants receive their primary economic support from secular employment.

Many women are employed by church agencies other than parishes: 16 per cent of the women priests and 11 per cent of the women deacons serve in church related positions. The largest group within this category is that of chaplain—to hospitals (41 ordained women), colleges and universities (23), primary and secondary schools (14), prisons (5), and nursing homes (12).[4] In Salt Lake City, Cheryl Moore is the chaplain at Westminster College; Linda Harrell has been chaplain at the University of Oregon since 1980. In Providence, Rhode Island, Flora Keshgegian is one of three chaplains appointed by Brown University. Andrea Smith serves as chaplain at Fairfield Hills Hospital in Connecticut; Judy Liro works as a part-time chaplain in a retirement center in Austin, Texas. Constance A. Hammond is the Refugee/Immigration Ministry coordinator with offices at Old North Church, Boston, Massachusetts.

Only one woman, Geralyn Wolf, serves as the dean of a cathedral—Christ Church Cathedral in Louisville, Kentucky. But 16 women serve as canons and 11 as assistants on cathedral staffs. Carole Anne Crumley has been canon pastor at the National

Cathedral in Washington, D.C., since 1982, a position that includes counseling, arranging weddings and baptisms, and ministering to "walk-ins." Catherine McKelvey is canon pastor of Christ Cathedral in Houston, Texas. Carla Berkedal is canon of St. Mark's Cathedral in Seattle, Washington. In addition, a number of women hold the position of honorary canon but do not list this position as their primary means of employment.

Forty-one clergywomen work as diocesan staff members—as archdeacons, canons, program directors, missioners and counselors with specific responsibilities. Becky Lepley and Cally Irish both serve as archdeacons in the Diocese of Michigan while Anne Garrison is assigned by that same diocese to minister to the gay community. Denise Haines is archdeacon for missions and urban ministry in the Diocese of Newark. As a deacon, Josephine Borgeson has served as the ministry development officer of the Diocese of Nevada for many years and has been a champion for the recovery of diaconal ministries. Six clergywomen work on the staff of the national church: priests Frances Nunn and Jane Rockman with the Presiding Bishop's Fund; Sheryl Kujawaa, Youth Office, and Elizabeth Turner in the Ecumenical Office; and deacons Lynn Coggi in Ministry with AIDS and Barbara Taylor in Ministries with Children.

Nine ordained women currently serve on seminary faculties and seven women serve in other staff positions in seminaries. (Several non-ordained women also serve as seminary faculty and staff members.) Among the priests on seminary faculties are Margaret A. B. Guenther, who directs General Seminary's Center for Christian Spirituality; I. Carter Heyward (theology) and Suzanne Hiatt (patoral theology) at Episcopal Divinity School; Rachel Hosmer (spiritual direction) and Patricia Wilson-Kastner (homiletics) at General Theological Seminary; Martha Horne (Greek) at Virginia Theological Seminary, and Eleanor McLaughlin (church history) at Andover Newton Theological School. Among the women priests with seminary staff positions are Rachelle Birnbaum, dean of students at the Church Divinity School of the Pacific; Martha Horne, and Sandra Boyd, director of public services at the Princeton Theological Seminary Library.

Some clergywomen continue to find their primary means of support in secular employment, often working with a local parish on a non-stipendiary basis on Sundays. Emily Hewitt is an attorney in Boston, Massachusetts; Anne Brewer is a physician in Hartford, Connecticut. Barbara Akin is a professor of history at Grove City College in Pennsylvania. Ten per cent of the women priests and 12 per cent of the women deacons are secularly employed.

Two per cent of women priests and seven per cent of women deacons are retired. Even after official retirement, however, many of the ordained women continue to carry out distinctive ministries. Ida Pettiford, for example, retired from a lifelong career as a social worker to go to seminary and be ordained. She then worked for the Diocese of Michigan as the assistant for urban affairs until she reached the mandatory retirement age of 72. She is now an unpaid assistant at a local church.

An overwhelming number of Episcopal clergywomen identify themselves as caucasian. At least twelve black women have been ordained including Barbara Harris, the executive director of the Episcopal Church Publishing Company, and Sandra Wilson, rector of St. Augustine's Church in Asbury Park, New Jersey. Among the women priests who identify themselves as Hispanic are Nina Alazraqui, who serves as vicar of St. Alban's Church in California, and Carmen Guererro, who returned from missionary service in Honduras and is now vicar of Santa Fe Mission in San Antonio, Texas. Dorothy Nakatsuji, of Japanese ancestry, is a permanent deacon who directs the ministry training program of the Diocese of Hawaii. Chinese-American Fran Toy is the alumni/ae coordinator at the Church Divinity School of the Pacific. Native American Anna Frank is rector of St. Matthew's Church in Fairbanks, Alaska, while Ruth Potter (Crow Creek Sioux) serves as a deacon in South Dakota.

Employment comparison

One means to study the acceptance of ordained women within the Episcopal Church is to compare their employment statistics with those of clergymen. In order to obtain comparable data bases, this section uses the files of the Church Deployment Office which includes only the records of those people who have submitted their personal profiles. Registered with this office are 610 women and 9,505 men—of a total of 14,482 ordained clergy as listed in the 1987 *Episcopal Church Annual*. Thus, only 69 per cent of all ordained clergymen and 56 per cent of all ordained clergywomen were registered with the Church Deployment Office as of June, 1987.[5]

This study compares the present employment of only those men and women ordained after January 1, 1977, the date the General Convention resolution allowing ordination of women to the priesthood took effect. By so doing, consideration is focused on men and women with comparable years of experience as priests—an important factor in the attainment of more responsible positions. As the following chart indicates, however, women still lag far behind men in being employed as rectors or vicars—from the CDO list of people ordained after 1976, 46 per cent of the men and only 19 per cent of the women today serve as rectors or vicars. Conversely, women are far more likely to be employed as assistants--43 per cent of the women and 34 per cent of the men work as assistants in congregations. A higher percentage of women serve as chaplains—in hospitals, schools, prisons or other institutions—9 per cent of the women and 4 per cent of the men. There is little deviation between the percentages of men and women filling the remaining job categories. It is interesting, though statistically insignificant, that the only person ordained after 1976 who serves today as dean of a cathedral is a woman—Geralyn Wolf. Only three persons in this group have been elected bishop— Leopold Frade (Honduras), Sturdie Wyman Downs (Nicaragua) and Charles Irving Jones, III (Montana).

Current deployment of women and men ordained after January 1, 1977 who are registered with the Church Deployment Office

RECTOR/VICAR (includes rectors of parishes and vicars of missions)

19% of all clergywomen
ordained after 1/1977

46% of all clergymen
ordained after 1/1977

ASSISTANT/ASSOCIATE (Includes specialized assistants such as pastoral counselors or Christian education as well as cathedral staff members)

46% of all clergywomen
ordained after 1/1977

36% of all clergymen
ordained after 1/1977

SUPPLY/INTERIM (Persons doing supply or interim work in parishes or missions)

8% of all clergywomen
ordained after 1/1977

5% of all clergymen
ordained after 1/1977

CHAPLAINS (Includes persons serving as chaplains at hospitals, military units, universities, schools, prisons, and other institutions)

9% of all clergywomen
ordained after 1/1977

4% of all clergymen
ordained after 1/1977

SECULAR EMPLOYMENT (Includes persons working for secular employers, directors of non-church agencies, and consultants)

5% of all clergywomen
ordained after 1/1977

2% of all clergymen
ordained after 1/1977

OTHER (Specialized ministries, religious orders, overseas missionaries, diocesan staff persons, teachers in church and non-church schools, students in seminaries and graduate schools)

13% of all clergywomen
ordained after 1/1977

7% of all clergymen
ordained after 1/1977

SOURCE: Search X427Y-M, X427Y-F, Church Deployment Office, 15 June 1987

Geographical distribution of ordained women

In terms of geographical distribution, ordained women are canonically resident in ninety-four of the ninety-eight domestic dioceses. The dioceses that have no ordained women are: Easton, Eau Claire, Fond du Lac, Quincy, and Springfield. Several other domestic dioceses have women deacons but no women priests. These are: Albany, Fort Worth, Georgia, Long Island, Louisiana, Nebraska, Northern Indiana, San Joaquin, Southwest Florida, Western Kansas and Western Louisiana. (See map on page 25.) Though data on many of the overseas dioceses is unavailable, there is one woman priest in both Central and South Mexico and Panama.[6] The absence of women priests in a diocese does not necessarily mean that diocese is closed to women priests. The present bishops of Easton, Georgia, Louisiana and Western Kansas have all indicated that they would ordain qualified women candidates.

The widespread distribution of women priests throughout the United States is even more evident in a provincial comparison. The percentage of all clergy who are women ranges from five to eleven per cent while the percentage of priests who are women ranges from two through eight per/cent. Province IV (Southeastern United States) has the lowest percentage of clergywomen, while the highest percentage are found in Province I (the New England States) and Province VI (the Northern Rockies and Plains States).

THE EPISCOPAL CHURCH

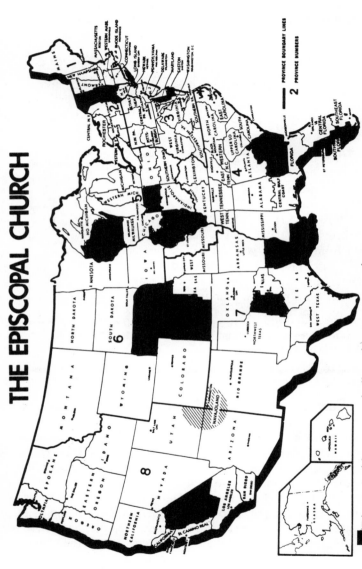

■ Dioceses with no canonically resident women priests

Distribution of ordained women by province as of January 1, 1987

	Women Clergy	Total Clergy	% of Total Who are Women	% of Priests Who are women
Office				
*Province I	156	1463	11%	8%
Province II	160	2124	8%	6%
Province III	172	2082	8%	7%
Province IV	106	2351	5%	2%
**Province V	143	1813	8%	6%
***Province VI	77	787	10%	7%
****Province VII	81	1462	6%	3%
*****Province VIII	189	2223	9%	6%

*Data from previous year for Connecticut.

**Data from previous year for Ohio.

***Data from previous year for South Dakota.

****Data from previous year for Oklahoma.

*****No data for Northern Luzon.

SOURCE: Episcopal Church Center, *Compilation of Annual Diocesan Reports, 1986* (as of September 4, 1987) Information available for Province IX (Central and South America) is incomplete.

Clergywomen on national church councils

Some women priests have been actively involved in the political life of the Episcopal Church. The number of women priests elected to represent their dioceses in the General Convention has risen each triennium. Five women served as clerical deputies in 1979, 7 in 1982 and 22 in 1985. Thirty-five women have been elected as clerical deputies to the 1988 General Convention as of December 8, 1987.[7] Several of these women deputies have served on significant committees of the General Convention. Ann Coburn is co-chair of the Joint Standing Committee on Program, Budget and Finance; Carol Anderson served for several years on the

Committee on the State of the Church, and is currently on the Joint Commission on Evangelism and Renewal. Other clergy-women and their committee assignments are: Daphne Hawks, Church Music; Anna Frank, Church in Small Communities; Rachelle Birnbaum, Constitution and Canons; Jane Garret, Peace; Sally Peterson and Patricia Wilson-Kastner, Ecumenical Relations; M. Barbara Akin, Examining Chaplains; and Helen Havens, Theological Education.

One woman priest, Sandra Wilson, and a deacon, Ruth Potter, serve on the Executive Council, the national body which has administrative oversight of the Episcopal Church between General Conventions. Many women priests are members of diocesan standing committees and commissions on ministry and serve in numerous other elected and appointed positions.

Conclusion

The acceptance of ordained women in the Episcopal Church has been widespread. In the past ten years, a substantial number of women have been ordained priest. These priests have been employed in a wide variety of positions throughout the church; their talents are enriching the church in every aspect of its life and work. Thousands of lay members of calling committees and vestries have considered various candidates as rectors and made the decision to call women priests to those positions.

Some inequities and examples of gender-discrimination remain. The comparison between ordained men and women with equal years of experience shows that women are chosen more often for subordinate positions in parishes rather than as rectors or vicars. Geographical distribution statistics indicate a markedly lower percentage of clergywomen in the southeastern states. There continue to be a few bishops who refuse to ordain or accept women priests in their dioceses, but their number has steadily diminished.

The overall pattern indicates that a social revolution of tremendous significance has moved through the church with relative ease. Photos from seminary catalogs show lively seminars of women and men learning from each other. Clergy conferences are no longer all-male bastions. Pregnant women preach from the pulpit.

Ordained sisters celebrate the Eucharist in convent chapels. Congregations across the country struggle with the problem of how to address a woman rector. Given the resistance to change generally present in organized religious institutions such as the Episcopal Church, the scope of the movement of ordained women into the life of the church over the last ten years has been remarkable.

Footnotes

1. Since printed Episcopal Church reports rely on data from the previous calendar year, these figures (which include 1987 ordinations) are from the data bank kept by two clergywomen, Sandra Hughes Boyd of Princeton Theological Seminary and Suzanne Hiatt of the Episcopal Divinity School. By reviewing diocesan newspapers and seminary publications, and corresponding with an informal network of clergywomen across the country, they have assembled the most current data available on ordained women. Sandra Hughes Boyd and Suzanne R. Hiatt, "Episcopal Clergywomen: Position Placement Statistics," 1 November 1987.

2. Totals from the overseas dioceses (Province IX and the Extra Provincial and Territorial Jurisdictions) are not included here. Episcopal Church Center, *Compilation of Annual Diocesan Reports, 1986* (as of 20 October, 1987).

3. Throughout this chapter, the figures used for the number of members of any given church are from *The Episcopal Church Annual,* 1987 (Wilton, CT: Morehouse-Barlow, 1987). Statistics on the numbers of women priests are from the *Compilation of Annual Diocesan Reports, 1986,* op. cit.

4. Overall percentages from ibid. Figures on the number of women in each category from Boyd and Hiatt, op. cit.

5. David L. Seger, Church Deployment Office, to Mary S. Donovan, 4 June 1987. The percentages of men and women registered are based on the numbers listed in the *Compilation of Annual Diocesan Reports, 1986.* For women, 610 of 1081 ordained women are registered. For men, the number of bishops (272) and the number of overseas clergy (385) must be added to the total number of domestic clergy (13,745). Of this number, 9,505 are registered with the Church Deployment Office. Church Deployment Office, Search X427Y-M, X427Y-F, 15 June 1987.

6. The statistics on geographical distribution are from *Compilation of Annual Diocesan Reports, 1986.* Reports from Connecticut, Ohio, South Dakota, Oklahoma, and Northern Luzon were not yet in so data from the previous calendar year (1985) was used for those dioceses. Very little information from the dioceses of Province IX was available. Information from overseas dioceses in other provinces (e.g. Haiti in Province II) is included in these comparisons.

7. *General Convention Journals,* 1979, 1982, 1985. Figures on the clergywomen elected deputies for 1988 convention from Diana Morris, General Convention Office, December 8, 1987.

Vienna Anderson with Bishop John Walker at her ordination to priesthood

Vienna Cobb Anderson

For those who do not yet believe, and for those who have lost their faith, that they may receive the light of the Gospel, we pray to you, O Lord.

The Litany for Ordinations

"The theatre was the best theological education I had, for it taught me to rejoice in God's handiwork and to seek re-creation in every setting. It taught me to own the pain and sorrow as well as the joy—and that both are essential to the growth of my being. It also taught me to be vulnerable. I could never create if I cut off my vulnerability. Vulnerability is connected to humility and love, to empathy and compassion, to depth of relationship with woman, man, child and God. Hence I do not seek perfection in work, play or liturgy—but vulnerability. Perfection is related to death, vulnerability to life.''

In a joyous celebration on April 11, 1987, the congregation of St. Margaret's Church in Washington, D.C., instituted their new rector—Vienna Cobb Anderson. Friends from throughout the diocese joined the celebration—former parishioners from St. Stephen and the Incarnation and St. Alban's Church where Anderson had served as associate rector, faculty and students she had taught at Virginia Theological Seminary, colleagues from the Hospice of Washington and members of the Community of Hagar, a group which she had helped found three years earlier. The intense dramatic quality of the liturgy, the vigor and excitement of the congregational responses and the pervasive joy that beamed from the faces of the participants all signaled that here, a special event was taking place. The parish had chosen well by calling Vienna Anderson to be their rector.

The position was challenging. The former rector had been asked to leave and the interim ministry had been difficult. "When I arrived," said Anderson, "membership had dropped considerably, energy was low, and the parish was dipping heavily into its endowment for general operating expenses." Beginning her work just before Lent, she was beset with planning Lenten and Easter services, her own institution and the bishop's annual visitation just after Easter. She had brought a new organist with her and together they sparked a new energy and excitement in the liturgy, inspiring the laity to new possibilities and new beginnings.

"It felt as though everything was starting at once and everyone wanted my time and attention immediately. There was never enough time to go around and too many meetings and late days and nights," she admitted. Financial problems were paramount—complicated by the immediate resignation of the treasurer and the discovery that the parish books had not been balanced for two years. Recruiting and training an efficient staff was a major focus of the first six months.

"One other aspect of my work has been to identify the current lay leadership of the parish and to support and nurture those people, discover new leaders, and identify the 'old guard' leadership," she added. "There are over forty shut-ins in the parish and I've spent a goodly amount of time calling on them and on those in the hospital."

By the end of 1987, St. Margaret's was a transformed parish. Attendance at Sunday services had doubled; pledged income was up from $108,000 to $148,000. Most parishioners increased their pledges and over fifty new pledges were made. An assistant priest, Herbert McMullin, was hired part-time. Church members had taken responsibility for developing new programs. The vestry committed a tithe of the parish's pledged income to outreach. The outreach committee formulated a theological perspective to guide the expansion of their efforts. Presently the parish sponsors one of the two D.C. sites for Amnesty (obtaining citizenship papers for immigrants) and is working to enlarge the Senior Citizens' Lunch Program in the parish hall. "The liturgy has become alive. The music program, under the direction of William Huckaby, is tremendous. And the people of the church are involved in the ministries of outreach. It's exciting to see," admitted Anderson.

The first year, though, was not without difficulties. Most painful to Anderson was the disagreement over use of the church by Dignity, a Roman Catholic organization of gay men and lesbians. Dignity had been holding weekly worship services at a chapel at Georgetown University but were asked to leave because of a Vatican policy discouraging formal ministries to such groups. Anderson, with the consent of the vestry and the approval of Bishop John T. Walker, allowed the group to hold services at St. Margaret's on Sunday evenings. Upset over this decision, a few parishioners petitioned the vestry to prohibit the Dignity services, which the vestry refused to do. "It's been very frustrating, trying to handle the anger and the pain of those who objected while letting them hear the basis for what we have done. How do you turn the problem around and not let it become destructive of the people involved or of the parish?" asked Anderson.

Paramount among resources that Anderson could draw on in this situation was her willingness to acknowledge her own vulnerability. Her religious journey had been a difficult one. "I knew as a child that I was to be a priest," she explained. "I knew in a right-brain way even though, according to logic, that was impossible." For she grew up in Richmond, Virginia in the forties in a very traditional Episcopal Church. "When I was eleven years old I told my rector that worship in the church according to the definition which he had taught me was a lie—he had taught me that worship was to love God with all my heart, body, mind and soul. But all he allowed us to do was say 'Amen.' The choir did the rest," Vienna added; "I left the church soon after that incident."

Attending Briarcliff Junior College and later the Yale School of Drama, she discovered acting, instead, as a place to use her whole heart, body, mind and soul. After further training, including a Fulbright scholarship to the London School of Music and the Dramatic Arts, she worked as a professional actress at the Barter Theater in Abingdon, Virginia; the Virginia Museum Theater in Richmond and later in New York in Broadway productions. But a persistent spiritual nagging—"I realized that while my friends were reading mysteries and love stories for recreation, I was reading theology!"—finally drove her to seek theological education.

Her attempt to achieve that education was filled with frustration. In the fall of 1963 when few Episcopal seminaries admitted women, she enrolled in one that did—Seabury-Western in Evanston, Illinois. But an acute infection led to hospitalization and she eventualy withdrew from the school, planning to transfer to Virginia Theological Seminary which had just opened its doors to women.

Since she had already arranged to do field work that summer at St. Bartholomew's Church in Richmond, she went ahead with that plan. There she found the field work was structured differently for women than for men. "The male seminarian was permitted to preach five times. I was allowed to preach once! When he complained about having to preach, I'd tell him to shut up or I'd take it away from him." At the final evaluation conference for all field work students, "I was treated abominably. Everyone talked down to me. When I objected to being treated like a second-class Christian, one man told me, 'You must remember, Vienna, there is a difference between priests and other Christians.' 'What difference?' I asked. 'I can celebrate the Eucharist and you can't,' the priest replied. I snapped back, 'You can't celebrate the Eucharist without me!' And then there was silence. Though some of the other seminarians tried to console me, it didn't help. It had been a horribly lonely and earth-shattering week.''

Though she'd planned to enter Virginia Seminary in the fall, the summer's experience had confronted her with the reality that she was not welcome in the ordained ministry. "My world had collapsed. All the props and walls that had secured and defined me had fallen away. I was like an onion, the circles had been pealed away to the center, I was at the core of myself. I was afraid there'd be nothing there. Instead I discovered a spark of love. It was all I had, but it was indeed a pearl of great price. It was hellishly painful but at the same time, incredibly free. I have often longed to be so free of defenses and props again."

Stripped of defenses, she allowed others to take over. It was her father who rescued her, suggesting a trip for them both. "The journey through Egypt, Jordan, Israel, Greece and Turkey was a rebirth, a holy journey," she said. She returned refreshed, at peace with herself and ready to go back to the world of the theater. She finished her M.F.A. degree in drama at Yale and taught speech and drama for the next three years at the District of Columbia Teachers' College, a predominantly black college. "Knowing nothing of blacks, I decided it would be impossible to live in this day and age so ignorant of a significant community in our nation. I took the job and learned much more than I taught."

After living for awhile in Reston, Virginia, Anderson moved into Washington, D.C., and joined the parish of St. Stephen and the Incarnation, a wonderful, yeasty place under the creative leadership of Bill Wendt. "St. Stephen's was the perfect place for my creative talents and liturgical experimentation," she recalled. "In the bleak days after my father's death, it was Bill Wendt and Priscilla Newell who got me through that time and Joyce Morfit who provided me with a new family." Encouraged to develop her own talents, she designed and fabricated liturgical vestments; her innovative designs combining varied colors, textures and fabrics added a powerful visual dimension to liturgical services.

The artistic outlet which her design work provided led Anderson to focus once again on theology. "In a sense, I stitched my way back into the church," she said, explaining how supportive the combination of art and theology was for her. Ready to renew her study, in 1969 she applied to be a candidate for holy orders in the Diocese of Washington. For the next eight years she encountered one roadblock after another; but eventually she was accepted as a candidate and enrolled in the Special Preparation for Ministry Program of the Diocese of Washington. Ordained deacon in June, 1977, she was ordained priest the following February. She did her field work at St. Alban's Church and stayed there after ordination, eventually becoming associate rector.

For Vienna, the seven years at St. Alban's were a period of integrating the rebelliousness of her current life with her Richmond heritage. "At St. Stephen's I had enjoyed the sixties life style—bright colors, long hair, long dresses, turtle neck sweaters and jeans, pillows on the floor instead of chairs. Moving to St. Alban's, I bought a house in D.C. and sent for the eighteenth century furniture I'd inherited and mixed it with pillows and a hammock in the living room. Changes within and without. I was learning to effect change from within the institution."

In 1982 when St. Alban's rector, A. Theodore Eastman, became bishop coadjutor of Maryland, Anderson stayed with the parish through the interim period and then resigned after the new rector arrived. She found herself facing a problem similar to that of many clergywomen—the difficulty of moving from being an assistant to being in charge. Her qualifications were excellent: she was a priest with seven years' experience in one of the busiest parishes in the nation's capitol. Before ordination, she had had twenty years' experience as a professional actress and teacher. Her education included a Fulbright scholarship in England and a degree from Yale. And yet, though she was considered by several calling committees and even offered the rectorship of one parish, only to have the offer rescinded two days later, she could not find a position.

Since she had become increasingly interested in ministry to the sick and dying, she decided to develop her skills in this area. To combine both practical experience with intellectual discipline, she began to work part-time as a chaplain at the Hospice of Washington and concurrently enrolled in a doctoral program at Princeton Theological Seminary.

"My mother agreed to subsidize me while I worked on my doctorate," Anderson said. "It was a hard thing for one who has struggled all her life to prove her independence to accept. But it was a good learning experience; I accepted and struggled with the feelings of dependency and incompetence that resulted from accepting her gift. And I was grateful."

Once again, Anderson's creative impulse turned adversity into a challenge. With her own feelings of dependency and rejection sharpening her awareness of those emotions in others, she became concerned about the unchurched. "Rather than sit around waiting for a job, I decided to create my own while I worked on my doctorate at Princeton." She called some friends together and, at a Eucharist celebrated on Pentecost, 1984, the Community of Hagar was born as "a group that would seek the outsider, care for the forgotten and explore feminist theology in search of new and inclusive, egalitarian ways to be the Body of Christ."

"Using 'An Order of Celebrating the Eucharist' from *The Book of Common Prayer,* we evolved our worship. Gathering became very important. Knowing the stranger in our midst was essential. Intimacy became central from the start—worshiping in a living room enhanced that. We sat in silence until someone was moved to read. Being led by the Spirit, waiting, listening became important and necessary elements of our worship. All responded, setting their lives in relationship with God's story. Our story and God's story became one."

As the liturgy evolved, the members began to seek ways to minister to the larger community. They outgrew Anderson's living room and rented a building for services. They visited the sick. As Sam Gillespie related, "When I was in the hospital last year, I had the effect of being cared for by this group in a way I had never been cared for before. Someone in the Community of Hagar was at the hospital every day for the month that I was there. And the gutsiness, the earthiness, the mundane, practical, nurturing, caring qualities of those men and women as they came to see me were something I attribute to Vienna's priesthood."

Today, though the Community of Hagar remains small, it has taken on a large-scale ministry to the families of victims of AIDS. Members continue to gather for worship each Sunday and to invite others into their midst. They are currently forming a support network for women in transition—those facing changes in jobs, marital status, or physical or mental health.

After three years with the Community and completing her doctorate at Princeton, Anderson was called to be rector of St. Margaret's. Though she hated to give up her association with the Community, she knew that the power she found there would remain. "We continually are presented with the opportunity to be transformed," she said. "That's God's way. And I knew I was being called to a new life. My leaving Hagar would open up the opportunity for transformation for them. St. Margaret's had entered into the transformation process by taking the risk of calling me. I knew I would be transformed by the new responsibilities awaiting me. So much new life seemed like a sure sign that this call was what God intended for me. All that I had learned and discovered needed to be tested in the heart of the institutional church and not just on the fringe. I needed to be at the center for a change."

Photo: Andrew Kilgore

Peggy Campbell Bosmyer

Will you persevere in prayer, both in public and in private, asking God's grace, both for yourself and for others, offering all your labors to God, through the mediation of Jesus Christ, and in the sanctification of the Holy Spirit?

The Examination

"It was at the General Convention in Louisville that women's ordination became a theological imperative for me," said Peggy Bosmyer. "Ordination was converted from a personal call to a total church issue for me, mostly because of all the negative arguments. The arguments against it were so horrendous, so theologically incorrect, so opposite of anything I had ever been taught from the time I was a cradle Episcopalian, that I had to fight. It was the Episcopal Church I was fighting for.''

Peggy Bosmyer is a slight, dark-haired woman with sparkling brown eyes. Watching her work with the senior counselors at Camp Mitchell, the diocesan conference center in Arkansas, one might have difficulty distinguishing which of those present was the priest. Yet, her youthful appearance belies the fact that she has been a priest since January, 1977. Indeed, she was one of the first women ordained to the priesthood after the General Convention action in 1976.

She serves today as vicar of St. Michael's Mission in Little Rock. St. Michael's is a suburban congregation with a unique focus on Christian commitment. ''The people at St. Michael's are involved, with one another, in the community, the diocese, and beyond. There are not very many passive people at St. Michael's,'' said parishioner Madge Brown, whose own involvement has included chairing the Arkansas Hunger Project and the Episcopal Church Women's national United Thank Offering Board. The congregation is small—about 150 baptized members—and though it includes a wide age range, its young married couples are producing babies at a prodigious rate. Bosmyer and her husband, Dennis Campbell, are part of the baby boom with a two-year old son, Michael, and a baby daughter, Lauren.

Madge Brown talked about Bosmyer's call to St. Michael's: ''As I showed a new visitor around the church last week, he asked me, 'Was Peggy Bosmyer put here because you were a mission and now you can't get rid of her?' And I looked at him and thought, what a funny conclusion or assumption to make. Because nothing could be any farther from the truth! We called Peggy to be our priest—even before women could be ordained priest. When our vicar resigned in 1976, we asked Bishop Christoph Keller if it would be possible for us to call Peggy. He just lit up like a Christmas tree. 'You know I cannot ordain her until I have a place to put her. I would be absolutely delighted, if there is a match there.' So we looked at her, and others, and decided she definitely was the best candidate. The senior warden, however, called every member of the congregation to ask what they thought about having a woman priest. No one was opposed. Some people said, 'I won't know how I would feel with a woman priest until I experience having one, but I am willing to try the experience.'"

As soon as the General Convention acted, St. Michael's issued the call. They also decided to wait with her, not celebrating the Eucharist (except for Christmas Eve), until she was ordained. That added a special dimension to the ordination service on January 29, 1977 when priest and people celebrated together her priesthood.

When asked what they liked best about Bosmyer's leadership, parishioners generally agreed it is her preaching. "Her sermons are very personal, yet timely, rooted in the gospel, attractive, touching," said one woman. "I almost always feel that she is speaking directly to me, where I am at that particular moment," said another. Not only the sermons, but also all the worship life of the congregation is crafted with great care; "There is a strong sense of the Holy Spirit in that place," reflected one person. The place is actually a former plumber's shop, attractively remodeled according to a design drawn up by a parishioner, Glenn Cox, and executed by another member, Bill Sneed. "We have simply never felt that we wanted to make the kind of expenditure from our budget that the construction of a new church would entail," Bosmyer explained. "We want to put our money to work out in the world."

The congregation is administered with a strong sense of shared leadership. "Peggy is always open to new ideas and never ever threatened by a person's desire to do anything," said Madge Brown as she described the congregation's new volunteer program. She and others interviewed each parishioner to discover what kind of volunteer activities they wanted to be involved in, what skills they had to offer, and what other kind of commitments (job, family, other voluntary positions) they had. Findings were entered on the computer and volunteer jobs were then assigned based on the information, each job with no more than a one-year term of service. The interviewing itself brought out new ideas—a cooperative parents' night out where two couples in turn would care

39

for all the babies each Friday night. "Do you want to do that?" the interviewer asked. "Oh, I'd be glad to set it up if others are interested."

Bosmyer sees the volunteer program as a way to get many tasks done and as a means to authenticate each person's ministry. "We've got some new people involved whom we would *never* have thought to ask to do the things they are doing."

"Peggy has a wonderful effect on men," said former senior warden Merry Helen Hedges. "She has really guarded against St. Michael's having the image of being an 'all-woman-run enterprise.' So she has called forth men from the congregation to assist her. I think that probably if you look at St. Michael's you would see an unusually high percentage of really active men." Men such as Earl Hillard who served as senior warden and organizes and coordinates the Sunday morning services, or Chuck Letzig, a recent convert who is already an active member of the vestry, appreciate the opportunity to assume leadership roles.

Little in Bosmyer's background would have predicted such a revolutionary step as her becoming one of the first women priests. She grew up in Helena, Arkansas, a small town located in the midst of rich delta land on the Mississippi River. By some quirk of fate, that community produced two of the main protagonists in the women's ordination struggle: Henry Rightor, professor of pastoral theology at Virginia Theological Seminary, who, as the secretary of the Joint Commission on Ordained and Licensed Ministers, became a key spokesman in favor of ordaining women in the early 1970s, and John Maury Allin, presiding bishop, who was opposed. Though she was of a later generation, Peggy Bosmyer attended St. John's Church with the families of both men.

That church became especially important to Peggy when her father died after a five-year battle with cancer. "I was dealing with all the kinds of things you normally deal with as a child when you are dealing with death. Some of it was guilt, some of it was anger at him and shame of him. There was just a huge gap in my life and I was looking for something that could fill it up. I remember sitting in church one day and hearing scripture,

'Visit the widows and the fatherless,' and I thought, 'That's me, the fatherless!' and I realized, 'This is where I can come. This is where I belong.'"

So the church became the source of stability in her adolescent world with the Reverend Phil Leach as a father figure. She was active in the youth group and dated a young man whom Leach was trying to recruit for seminary. "I would tell Phil, I was the one who wanted to go to seminary, and he'd laugh and say, 'No, no, you can't be a priest; women can't be priests. You can be a nun.' But I didn't want to be a nun." This friendly banter continued until Bosmyer went off to college and, in her words, "left all of that junk way, way behind me."

Not until her last year at the University of Arkansas did she find her way back to church. Chaplain David Johnson (now bishop of Massachusetts) helped her deal with an emotional crisis and then continued to take her religious questions and interests seriously. Gradually, the idea of seeking further Christian education grew in her mind, and Johnson encouraged her to enroll in seminary, though she had no intention of being ordained, an idea rarely considered in 1971 when she graduated from college. She enrolled at Virginia Theological Seminary seeking a master of theological studies, a degree that did not lead to ordination.

Bosmyer entered seminary playing the role of a southern belle—submissive, demure, pious—carefully distinguishing herself from the few women there who were enrolled in the master of divinity program. Between her middler and senior year, she took clinical pastoral education at Massachusetts General Hospital in Boston, an experience that "was a real painful growing-up experience. For the first time in my life, there was a demand for me to be the person I knew I was, a demand to give up the survival game I was playing. I came back knowing that I wanted to work for the church full time. But I was still vehemently against my being ordained. Not against women's ordination, just the ordination of *this* woman."

The debate at the 1973 General Convention at Louisville convinced Bosmyer that the church, to be true to its own proclamation, had to open the priesthood to women. Returning to Virginia

Seminary, where she had moved to the master of divinity program that fall, she finished her senior year. After graduation she returned to Arkansas to be ordained deacon in August, 1974.

By 1976, St. Michael's had called her as vicar. "Coming home from the Minneapolis Convention, I flew into the Little Rock Airport," she said. And a huge crowd of people were there in the airport waiting area, with iced champagne and a huge sign, ALLELUIA, that went all across the front of the terminal. The whole lobby was just packed with people; Episcopalians cheering, and Roman Catholics too. Someone told us the Roman Catholic nuns had been praying for us all through the convention. Everybody in the airplane was going 'Wow, look at that! What's happening?' And we said, 'The Episcopal Church just voted to ordain women.' I was so proud to be an Episcopalian. The impossible had happened; you rarely ever change that much tradition in that short an amount of time. It was incredible. It's one of those things I'll probably tell my great-grandchildren about, if I live that long."

On January 29, 1977 Bosmyer was ordained priest. The service was not without pain for many people in the diocese who opposed the step. Charles Higgins, dean of Trinity Cathedral where the ordination took place, accepted an out-of-town speaking engagement so that he would not have to take part; his assistant, Richard Clark, spent the hours of the service taking communion to shut-ins. But for those present it was a joyous celebration.

Since the job at St. Michael's was only part-time, Bosmyer was also hired as diocesan youth coordinator and director of the summer camp program. Working with young people was a central concern for her. "I know that one of the reasons I am so committed to young people is because of what the church meant to me at that age," she said. She holds youth leaders in great respect, listening carefully to their suggestions and depending upon them to assume responsibility. "She was very demanding," said counselor Martin Fulk, "but at the same time, she was also very demanding of herself—made it a point to be available eighteen hours a day, both to the campers and to the counselors."

The youth work also had the serendipitous effect of introducing women's ordination to the entire diocese. "I was so visible at Camp Mitchell," Bosmyer remembered, "and had to deal with so many people from all over the state, that they all got used to the idea of a woman priest. Women clergy are just not an issue with most of our young people because I have been such an integral part of their diocesan church experience."

Her Camp Mitchell visibility became somewhat of a problem for Bosmyer four years ago when, in the midst of the summer camp session, she realized she was falling in love with Dennis Campbell whom she had hired as assistant camp director. Finally a perceptive laywoman simply arranged for the two to get away from camp by presenting Peggy a free dinner at an elegant French restaurant and ordering Dennis to escort her. "I knew they just needed some time without kids around so they could really talk," said Claudia Howe. "Peggy was trying to be so cool in her relationship to Dennis but we could all see what was happening." They were married that fall with counselors, staff members and campers from all across the diocese joining the festivities.

Marriage and then motherhood brought a new maturity and depth to Bosmyer's ministry. "We feel like we've been able to share the excitement of their marriage," said Madge Brown. "It's been wonderful to see the difference marriage has made in her. And we didn't worry about her having babies. There was no looking askance at a pregnant priest. You know, it seemed so natural; I don't know anybody who didn't just delight in that."

Marriage did mean an adjustment in her relationship with the congregation, Bosmyer admitted. "The congregation needed to learn that I had another, primary family, that they had become my secondary family whereas before, as a single priest, they were my primary family." She and Dennis deliberately scheduled time away from the church and began to make it clear that they did not have to attend every parish meeting and event. "I felt I had to fight for time with my family—but I had to do that for the parish's sake as much as for my sake. Priests must model the importance of family life, especially today, because there is so much in our world that does not support families."

Peggy's husband, Dennis, is also struggling with a call to

ordination. As a postulant for holy orders, he commutes each week to seminary in Memphis, Tennessee, a four-hour drive. Balancing family life, church commitments, and educational demands is difficult for the couple. The uncertainty of Dennis' position for the next few years is psychologically wearing on them both, but they feel they are blessed with strong support from St. Michael's Church. And both have a strong sense that they are in God's care. "Being a priest is something you do if you are called to do it," said Bosmyer. "It is not an easy life; but it is something that has to be God's decision for you. It is a gift."

Nancy L. Chaffee

*For you are the God of my strength; why have you put me from
you? and why do I go so heavily while the enemy oppresses me?*

Psalm 43, The Ordination of a Priest

"It is in the desert that we become worried enough about living
that we become dependent upon God to be fed, nourished, and
strengthened. It is then that we listen. I have also come to realize
that we have to retreat from the war in order to hear God. Our
desert experience involves struggle. And we, like Jacob, wrestle
with God in the night. When morning comes we find we are not
the same, we are wounded. But it is in touching our own wound-
edness that we seek to discover that we can go on the journey
with others who seek healing."

Nancy Chaffee speaks with such eloquence about struggle because it has been a central theme in her life. When she was born
with cerebral palsy in 1942, her parents were told she would
probably never walk or talk. Refusing to be governed by this
diagnosis, however, they expected their daughter to live as normally
as possible and she more than fulfilled those expectations. She
learned not only to walk, but to dance and roller skate; she played
the piano and the organ. Her maternal grandmother communicated
her own deep religious faith to the young girl. "She provided
hope, pointing always to Jesus, to the cross. She used to say that
God would use me just as I was. That stuck somewhere inside
of me, and was to be the motivating force in the days of despair."

Today Chaffee serves as the executive director of Disability
Awareness, an empowering ministry. Most of her work is in
preaching and conducting workshops to educate clergy, congregations, and parish communities about how to be inclusive of
persons with all kinds of disabilities. "For you see," she explains,
"our society is permeated with a silence about disability, a feeling
that if we don't talk about 'it,' 'it' will go away. My present work
is aimed at breaking that silence. My visibility in the church says

45

Nancy L. Chaffee

something about God at work in the lives of persons with disability. I preach about a subject many people don't want to discuss; I invite people to accept and to touch the unacceptable in life—to see that disability is not unique to a few, but rather that it is universal."

She sees that silence in families with disabled children. "It is the silence of shame, guilt, and fear. It hides the grief, the pain, and the struggle of both the family and the child. Perhaps it spares them from judgment and rejection by the church. But, more significantly, it *prevents* them from being part of a community. It eliminates a source of hope, strength and healing of the grief and the hurt."

She also feels the silence in adults with disabilities. "They don't know who they are. Since they do not know what it means to integrate the disability into their total personhood, they are often angry and drag their disability along to use as a weapon against others. The silence strands them in a spiritual wasteland." To break out of the wasteland, Nancy counsels people to begin by naming the problem—learning what the disability is and as much as possible about how it affects the individual. Her therapy is not easy; it is tough. It involves willingness to share and laugh and cry with each other. And it demands an openness to the possibility of the infusion of God's grace.

"Nancy's work and most especially her presence serve to strengthen and acknowledge the gifts of persons with disabilities," explained Joan McDonald, an audiologist who heads the Michigan disabilities task force. "She enables us to see a *whole person* rather than only a partial person. She herself is a living embodiment that we are *all* important to the functioning of the Body of Christ."

Though Chaffee's workday is generally occupied with programs for and about people with physical and emotional disabilities, her own understanding of priesthood is central to this work. Her offices are located at Grace Church in Elmira, N.Y., where she assists with worship services as her travel schedule permits. Previously she was priest-in-residence at St. David's Church in DeWitt, New York, celebrating the Eucharist and participating in the worship life of the congregation as much as her traveling schedule permitted.

She lives with her daughter, Melody, a high school senior. Daughter Lisa is twenty-five and lives independently. Like most single mothers, Nancy works too hard; the daily tasks of running a household along with the pressure of an intensive travel schedule place a heavy demand on her. "Melody is a marvelous help to me," she acknowledged, "but I try to be careful not to overburden her with caring for me. I am finally beginning to learn how to cut back, provide time for the tiredness, and provide more time to be home and reflect on where I've been."

Chaffee's journey toward priesthood was inextricably linked with her search for selfhood. From earliest childhood, she knew she was different from those about her. And when they named that difference "inferiority" she believed them. For her, the usual emotional swings of adolescence were complicated by the frustration of dealing with a world that generally focused upon her disability rather than upon the person. Though she read the familiar fairy tales of sleeping beauty and the handsome prince, she knew intuitively that the prince would not come to rescue her. He would just look past her on the street. She lived in a world somewhere outside the experience of her peers, hampered also by the fact that neither she nor her parents were ever given much factual information about cerebral palsy, its prognosis and symptoms. Not until she was in her thirties did she even meet another person with cerebral palsy. Her world told her that women should be gentle and non-combative and accepting, that they should seek marriage and children and fulfillment as homemakers. Nancy, like the young women around her, internalized those desires.

She married, against the advice of her parents and the objections of many friends, just out of high school. Looking back now on that union, she realizes that both she and her husband were working out personal insecurities, she by trying to prove that her disability would not prevent her from finding the American dream, he by trying to sublimate his own sense of helplessness by rescuing and taking care of her. They had two daughters, born eight years apart. Her pregnancies were normal and both deliveries were without complications. However, the frustration of dealing with a physician who was unwilling to speak frankly about cerebral palsy and its effect on pregnancy made the entire process much more difficult.

Early in their marriage, her husband began to drink heavily. The drinking led to increased brutality against her and the girls as well as growing hostility from his family who blamed Nancy's disabilities for his alcoholism. She felt trapped and insecure; her overtures for help were met with disbelief and blame. "My family believed that his abuse was my fault," she explained. "They thought I should be forever grateful that someone had even married me; it was my responsibility to make the marriage work at all costs." Finally convinced that the situation would not improve, she left him and sued for a divorce.

As a thirty-two-year old mother with two children, unable to find employment, she enrolled in a community college, planning to study creative writing, an occupation she could pursue at home. But she took one class in theology from a priest who recognized the person behind the handicap. He encouraged her work, and eventually helped her obtain a scholarship to Wells College, a private women's college in Aurora, New York. There she found "I was being treated as a capable, thinking adult. I was being taken seriously and was being encouraged to look for answers to the questions that troubled me." At the same time she discovered the Episcopal Church. "There was something there for me; the crucifixion was a powerful symbol of struggle, of suffering. But Easter was even more powerful as a symbol of triumph and of *hope*."

Tugging at the back of her consciousness since she was sixteen years old was a call to ministry. The confidence she gained at Wells enabled that call to surface once again. Eventually, she approached Bishop Ned Cole of Central New York, offering to serve as an unpaid sacramentalist with a specific ministry to the terminally ill. Cole refused the offer, urging her instead to go to seminary and seek priesthood through the regular channels.

She entered Bexley Hall Seminary (the Episcopal seminary affiliated with Colgate Rochester Divinity Schools in Rochester, New York). Seminary taught her to integrate her disability into her sense of herself, of her own personhood. As she explained, "I no longer had a need to be ashamed, or to feel that I was not in the image of God. Indeed, the discovery that I *was* in the image of God was very liberating. How long I had been taught that to be in the image of God meant to be white, male, middle-class and *perfect*. But God is not limited. Whatever we are, is what God is too, for God is not limited by our finite ideas of perfection."

"I was awed by the fact that even with cerebral palsy Nancy was able at most times to keep up with the class," said a fellow seminarian, Richard L. Twist. "It was awfully difficult for her to take notes at a desk that was not designed for someone with disabilities. Being able to write at a desk was something I'd taken for granted."

Chaffee spoke with gratitude of the people involved in her path toward priesthood. "Every member of the Commission on Ministry and the Standing Committee has been personally affirming of me and of my call, as well as having supported me collectively. Their evaluations never centered on what I could not do but rather on how *they* could assist *me* in developing my ministry. As a deacon, I served under the Reverend Wallace Frey at St. David's parish. They too were willing to work with me, to accept me, and to learn from me and with me."

Old forms and expectations had to be revised to cope with Nancy's disabilities. To celebrate the Eucharist, she works with a licensed chalice bearer who lifts and carries the elements. "The person reaches across the altar to accept the gifts of wine, water and bread. He then pours the wine and water into the chalice, with my hand merely resting atop his. He then carries the ciborium with wafers, and I take them one at a time to serve. I do not carry the paten since to do so might have the wafers spilt. The ciborium prevents that from happening." It is a slow, sometimes awkward process, and yet, as one couple related, watching Nancy distribute the bread suddenly broke open the Eucharist for them, interjected the dimension of Christ's suffering into their communion with transforming power. For her, the moment "was both an affirmation and acceptance. It was also a reminder that things which I often am embarrassed about are the very vehicle which God has chosen to express God's power and presence in my life, with and for others."

Being a woman is also important to her priesthood. She takes her femininity seriously. "I like to wear pink suits, pink stockings. I take care with my makeup and hairstyles. I like to wear bright color combinations with my clerical collar. Being a woman adds a very special dimension to my priesthood; it is important for me to affirm that dimension," she asserted. She is also concerned about other women clergy and has been gathering research data on a group of clergywomen and aspirants to the priesthood who have disabilities. "The issues and problems they face are staggering in terms of employment, pay, acceptance, insurance, being allowed to attend seminary and being accepted in the ordination process," she related. Part of her work today is to bring these issues to the attention of those who are able to influence the ordination process.

Life is still not easy for Chaffee. Each step of every day is taken with some difficulty. There continue to be periods of deep despair, spiritual wastelands that simply must be traversed. She has learned to be open with others, to speak about her own disability in a way that will encourage others to do the same. But that openness also leaves her vulnerable to pain. She still struggles with being a person who happens to live with a disability. She is also constantly frustrated with people who will not hear the message she proclaims: Christians who give lip service to compassion and ignore people with disabilities in their midst, churches that will spend thousands of dollars on a new organ but nothing on a ramp that would enable people in wheelchairs to enter to hear the music.

Yet, she has discovered inner strength. "I am awed by the grace of God which comes to me again and again as I struggle with many issues. I am awed that God uses something which I found difficult to accept as a means of power to speak to others who also wrestle with these same hurts. I am awed as a priest that the expectations I live through become the message of my sermons and that those words become a way of conveying the presence of God to others. All of this has caused me to continually search for a deeper spirituality that grows into God. That means that I do experience the desert in profound ways in that journey but I also experience a deeper awareness of the price to live out one's call in a ministry such as I have."

Ann Struthers Coburn with her father-in-law, Bishop John Coburn, and her husband, Michael Coburn

Ann Struthers Coburn

Will you do your best to pattern your life and that of your family in accordance with the teachings of Christ, so that you may be a wholesome example to your people?

The Examination

"It is a hard lesson for me to learn that I can't have it all—career, family, personal life—all the time. I am always learning to sacrifice and compromise and balance," admitted Ann S. Coburn—priest, rector (with husband Michael) of St. James' Church, Danbury, Connecticut, and mother of eight-year-old Noah and four-year-old Abigail. Since Ann and her husband share the rector's position, there is a tendency for church business to engulf their entire lives. "Fortunately our children are at a stage where they need attention; they prevent the dinner table talk from getting too church oriented. We often take the phone off the hook when we sit down to eat," she said.

The number of clergy couples—two ordained persons married to each other—is surprisingly high. Ann Coburn estimates there are at least 125 couples of Episcopal priests married to each other, as well as a number of Episcopal women priests who are married to clergymen of other denominations.

Though any two-career marriage is faced with difficult decisions and choices, two factors make life especially difficult for clergy couples. The first is deployment—there simply may not be two openings for priests in a given geographical area at the same time. Parishes are reluctant to take on a couple in a shared ministry. Couples who take on two different churches in one geographical area find their family life assaulted by conflicting loyalties. Second, a parish's sense of ownership of "our priest" often involves subtle (or not so subtle) control over that priest's private life. This might result in two parishes competing for control over one couple's family life or, if both priests work in the same congregation, an almost overwhelming sense, for the priests, of being "married" to that congregation, of never being able to get away from the concerns of the parish.

Ann and Michael Coburn met the problem of deployment by sharing one position; both were called as rector of St. James' parish. They each work part-time and share one full-time salary. "The parish probably gets the best of both of us," Ann pointed out, noting that such flexibility is possible since ministry has never been a nine-to-five job. How do they divide up responsibility? "Whoever is in the office is the one who makes immediate decisions," Ann related, "but I tend to be more concerned with financial matters and Michael with building and grounds. There are obviously decisions that must be considered jointly, but the parish seems comfortable with our style and the way we do things. We alternate presiding at vestry meetings."

St. James' is a large parish with an average Sunday attendance of about 350 people. There are two full-time assistants—a man and a woman—on the staff; and the four clergy constantly wrestle with better ways of implementing a team ministry. St. James' is an urban parish with an extensive outreach program—food pantry, homeless shelter, street ministry. Helping the parish claim ownership of these ministries is frustrating for Ann, but "when it works, there is much rejoicing in the kingdom."

Ministry with women is one important phase of Ann's work that has gradually evolved as she has worked at St. James'. Premarital counseling and working with parents and godparents before baptisms were often means to initiate conversations which continued long after the event had taken place. However, in the last two years, she has been leading more and more house groups and retreats for women. "Women are awakening to the need to work on their spiritual life," she said. "They want to study the Bible and try to relate that to where they are. A lot of these women are not necessarily struggling—it's not as if they are in crisis—but they are dealing with the realities of women in this stage of society. How can you be a superwoman—have a family and work full time and be perfect in every way? I think there's a myth out there that women can somehow do that; and women put that myth on themselves.

Allied with the search for spirituality is a greater openness, a freedom to make statements of faith to others. "One of the big things we do at St. James' is tell our stories," Coburn explained. "If you tell something about yourself, if you share your spiritual journey, it's very revealing. Others see you in a new light. That builds up friendships and bonds you to others in very special ways. That process has built a whole trust level that just wasn't here when we arrived."

How did Ann and Michael both find themselves in the ministry? Products of the sixties and the upheaval of the Vietnam war, they shared a common idealism about doing something for others. Marrying while in college, she worked as a teacher while he was a social worker in the New Jersey prison system after graduation. But somehow that wasn't enough. Something was missing in their lives. Entering seminary was at first more of a search for that missing element—a chance to explore the faith in which they both were raised. Michael's father, John B. Coburn (retired bishop of Massachusetts), at that time was president of the House of Deputies and rector of St. James' Church, New York City. So the young couple chose the Church Divinity School of the Pacific in Berkeley,

California as a symbolic way to get away from their east coast ties and "do our own thing."

They had chosen well. "We loved what we were doing and we thrived—as individuals and as a couple." Except for required courses, Ann and Michael tended to choose different electives, shaping their education to their personal interests. However, during their first summer, they took the clinical pastoral education course together at Pacific State Hospital in Pomona, California—a huge institution for the mentally retarded and developmentally disabled. "That was when our call to ordained ministry—together—really became clear to us. It was a real conversion for us," Ann explained. "Although we'd worked together, we had never really ministered together. We found we really enjoyed sharing that ministry."

Much harder, they found, was to get a diocese to hire them to work together in a team ministry. Bishops were afraid to accept clergy couples, seeing chiefly the potential problems they represented. After interviewing for several positions, the Coburns finally convinced St. James' parish to hire the two of them to fill the vacant curate's position. After two years there, they moved to share another job as canon at the cathedral, and then were called back to St. James as rector in 1982.

The difficulties they faced prompted them to reach out to other clergy couples. They have been active in developing a support network among such couples, currently serving on the Episcopal Couples' Steering Committee which put together a national conference in 1986. Forty-two couples, with their children, gathered at Stony Point, New York to share their common joys and frustrations. "The meeting was very affirming to the families, to the kids in particular. Some of the clergy couples are so isolated; they were delighted to find a place where they could sound off. We've continued to keep in touch through a newsletter and are planning another get-together at General Convention next year," Coburn explained.

Ann Coburn has also been extensively involved in the political life of the Diocese of Connecticut. She serves on the screening committee for the Commission on Ministry, is a member of the Cathedral Chapter and works with the Support Committee for

Ordained Women. The diocese has elected her as a deputy to the General Conventions of 1982, 1985 and 1988. She serves as the vice chairman of the Joint Standing Committee on Program, Budget, and Finance which formulates the church's national program for the succeeding triennium.

The Coburns are looking forward to a sabbatical leave at the beginning of 1988 when they, with their children, will spend three months in Zimbabwe, ministering to a congregation that has been without a clergyman for two years. Like much of Africa, Zimbabwe has an acute shortage of ordained clergy; the Diocese of Manicaland to which the Coburns are going has only about twelve clergymen for over three hundred congregations. They intend to serve chiefly as sacramentalists—bringing the sacraments to the Christians there—and to share with their children the experience of living in a different part of the world.

Since the diocese has not yet ordained women to the priesthood, Ann is not sure what her status will be there. "I recognize your call," Bishop Elizah Masuko told her, "and I am depending on the Holy Spirit to work this out for us." She suspects that her presence as a priest will be a means of testing the people's response to the possibility of ordained women. She hopes the African people, with their deeply ingrained sense of hospitality, will allow her to exercise her priesthood among them and she hopes that the communion they share will open new possibilities both for her and for them.

The Coburns' lives and ministries meet in extraordinary convergence. "Our greatest joy," said Michael Coburn, "is that there is so much unity in terms of the two areas of our life—professional and private—that we can be supportive of one another in both those arenas in very unusual ways." But he admitted that there is also a danger there—"The two arenas get so conflated that you can't separate out where you begin and your profession ends. The biggest drag of the whole thing is the daily scheduling; the greatest joy is in the sharing."

"We are excited about the challenge of our coming sabbatical leave," Ann Coburn said. "We, as well as the parish, need some time away in order to re-create and renew ourselves and our ministry. During this year, St. James' is conducting a capital campaign to renovate its worship and office space and make necessary repairs to the buildings. We know that will be an uphill climb—it's scary but necessary. And if we reach our goal, we will have brought this parish to a point of connectedness in terms of its worship, its community life, its outreach work and its presence in Danbury. I know from experience that St. James' Church is a richer place because there are two ordained women on the staff. In a time when women are struggling with career and family choices, this is a place where they can find someone who is struggling with them. The message we are giving out is that it's okay to be a woman in the church."

Phebe Lewald Coe

That she may faithfully fulfill the duties of this ministry, build up your Church, and glorify your Name, we pray to you O Lord.

The Litany for Ordinations

"What has become most important to me in my daily vocation is an on-going, still overpowering, sense of being in the right place and doing with my life the right thing. My experiences, successful and unsuccessful, all seem to be preparing me and making me ready for days ahead. I am most alive when I am pursuing my studies, my Sunday preparations, the pastoral work and preaching. My heart beats faster just to think of it. Some people call this experience a verification of their 'call.' I simply know that my desire to serve the church and to grow into 'the full stature of Christ' is a powerful drive that keeps urging me on and on."

In her tenth year as a clergywoman, Phebe Coe expressed the validity she finds in her call. Coe serves as the rector of Epiphany Church in Odenton, Maryland. Founded in 1917 as the Maryland World War I Chapel, Epiphany had remained a small village church for most of its life. Over the past few decades, it was served by a succession of part-time clergy. However, as suburban Baltimore and Washington, D.C., moved out to engulf the area around Odenton, the potential for membership growth became obvious. As a part of a plan to seek new members in the neighboring community, the church called Coe as rector. Though the position was part time, she accepted it, convinced that under her leadership the congregation could grow strong enough to support a full-time rector within a year. To supplement the part-time salary, she also serves as an Episcopal chaplain at the Johns Hopkins Hospital in Baltimore. That position was made possible by Bishop Theodore Eastman, who recognized Epiphany's growth potential and wanted to make the rectorship financially possible for Coe.

Coe is enthusiastic about her new parish. "Epiphany Church has a lot going for it," she said. "It had been struggling along with part-time priests for many years. I remember during my interview with the search committee, someone asked me, 'If my husband were to die, would you bury him or would you find someone else to do it?' In the past, the priests who have served this church have had other jobs which made it difficult to be with people other than at night or on weekends. As the question reveals, pastoral needs have not always been treated as important enough to come first." For Coe, the pastoral needs of the congregation have top priority.

She began with a fresh look at the church structure itself. "I recognized that under the aluminun siding was quite a unique and historically interesting building from the Arts and Craft Movement in America. Inside, I found a lovely example of that movement hidden behind bookcases and army green paint and banners and clutter that I attribute to years of part-time care. The building is a gem that the owners, or rather the stewards, did not know that they had."

Coe organized a series of clean-up days during which the people threw out the clutter, added fresh paint, trimmed and manicured the shrubbery outside and generally rehabilitated the external fabric. "You know, what we've needed around here for a long time has been a woman's touch," one parishioner proclaimed. The revitalized building gave a new sense of worth and pride to the congregation. "And with this 'stirring up' has come publicity and visibility and new interest. The congregation tripled in twelve weeks, Coe proclaimed. "I wouldn't choose any other church for me right now. After ten years as a priest, I have a wonderful opportunity to see and to learn what it really takes to build a congregation and to set it upon a good solid foundation."

Coe has a clear perception of what it will take to build the parish. Pastoral needs must come first. She is faithful about calling on the sick and the shut-ins, about ministering to people in times of special crisis. In addition, the worship life must be strengthened. She takes particular care in arranging the worship services every Sunday and spends a good deal of time on her

Phebe Coe outside Epiphany Church with (from left) Marie Ferguson Davie, Wesley Waters, Ray Phipps and Pauline Kimmett, and (left, rear) Cari Fretz, James Kimmett, Hilda Waters and Kathy Kimmett

sermons, seeing them as a way to reach out to newcomers and oldtimers alike. With an attentive ear to the unvoiced concerns of her flock, she has set up a schedule to visit every current member of the parish and every person who has been associated with the church in the past as well as those who appear in church for the first time.

Two days a week she drives the thirty miles to Johns Hopkins Hospital where she shares the position of chaplain with Doris Mote, another clergywoman working with a small parish. "I've found myself formulating a new definition of chaplaincy," she explained. "There are hundreds of Episcopalians working in all capacities at Hopkins; the chaplaincy must be, for them, a way to sharpen *their* ministry at Johns Hopkins Hospital, a ministry I share with them."

To symbolize that presence, Coe began a weekly ecumenical Eucharist open to support staff, families, doctors—"whoever happens to come." That service has become a way of forming a religious support network within the hospital.

Health care for AIDS victims is an area of particular concern for Coe. "Right now, in the entire state of Maryland, there are only four chronic-care beds designated for AIDS patients," she explained. "So through the Episcopal Social Ministries office we are putting together a workshop to talk specifically about continuity and total care, putting doctors and health care workers in touch with members of the wider community who are in a position to initiate change. Bringing church, staff, and community together around an area of common concern is part of what I mean by the redefinition of the work of a chaplain."

In this occupation, Coe draws upon a wealth of previous experience. She had served as the associate rector of Memorial Church in Baltimore, a midsized urban parish where she was much loved. According to Delia Doll, widow of the late bishop of Maryland, Harry Lee Doll, "Phebe is very sensitive to people and their needs. She has a quiet strength that is appealing and nonabrasive. Her spirit simply shines in her face—she is very lovely. Her mind is as lovely as her face. Her sermons are excellent. She is theologically sound and brings what I would call a consecrated imagination to what she says. I have seen a congregation really spellbound by her sermon and the new light she has brought them on a topic. She brings great enthusiasm to all she does but is willing and anxious to hear what ideas other people have. I cannot say too much about the quality of her ministry or her preaching."

Coe was especially attentive to the older people at Memorial Church, serving as chaplain to a nearby apartment house for the elderly where "their love for her was close to adoration." "The people of Memorial Church responded very positively to Phebe," said parishioner Alma Bell, "She quickly won over most of those who were opposed to the idea of female clergy."

Phebe Coe's interest in theology developed even before priesthood was possible for women in the Episcopal Church. As the daughter of a corporate executive, she lived in several cities in her early years. Though she had been baptized as a baby, church ties were not particularly important for her until she discovered religion classes at Goucher College. "I remember specifically feeling that

I *needed to know* the information from those classes. It was a matter of how I was going to live for the rest of my life," she explained.

Hungry for a more intensive religious education, Coe entered Union Theological Seminary in New York City in 1972. After two years there, she transferred to Seabury-Western Theological Seminary in Evanston, Illinois, where she received her master of divinity degree. She returned to the Diocese of Maryland and was ordained deacon in February, 1977, and priest at the end of that year by Bishop David Leighton. After two intern years at St. Bartholomew's Episcopal Church in Baltimore, she was hired as associate rector of Memorial Church, in the same city. The rector, Barney Farnham, admitted that he had some reservations about women clergy when he first hired Coe, but after working with her, he is adamant that he would never again direct a multiple staff that did not include at least one clergywoman.

Phebe and Cameron Coe were married in 1978 and their son, Samuel, was born while she was at Memorial. "When Phebe was pregnant, the congregation was delighted," said Mrs. Doll. "I think one of the most deeply moving experiences was a Christmas before her delivery, when, large with child, she came down into the nave to read the gospel. It was a moment of breathtaking beauty and meaning for me, and I think for many others, both men and women."

After ordination in the Lutheran Church of America and four years in the parish ministry, Cameron now teaches English at Severn School, a private high school. How does he handle being married to a priest? "Mostly by putting clear requests upon me about when I'm going to be home," she laughed. "Scheduling is our biggest problem!"

In 1982, the Diocese of Maryland elected Coe as one of their four clerical deputies to General Convention and she has been re-elected twice to that position. "I ran for the position because I thought that it was important to have both men and women priests in the delegation," she admitted, "but I was astounded by the convention, particularly by the amazing diversity of the people who served as deputies. It was a very powerful statement of the richness and inclusiveness of our Episcopal heritage. Seeing the potential there, I realized it was important to me to take an active part in that body and to bring the vision I saw there back to the diocese." Though she spent her first General Convention listening and learning, she has worked to develop the political skills and associations to become a very effective member of that parliament.

Whether hammering out the wording for a resolution for General Convention or counseling with a bereaved widow, Phebe Coe's special gift is "that she is truly called to serve," attested Bruce McPherson. "She regularly works miracles with people—enabling them, giving them hope, bringing new life to them, quietly, patiently, one at a time. In our relationship, Phebe was always able to pinpoint the source of my pain and ease it or the source of my joy and celebrate it. I highly value her counsel, her concern and her love."

Iva O'Neal Cutshaw with granddaughter Karie Lapetina, daughter Shirley Alt, grandson Curtis Cutshaw, son Jerry Cutshaw, daughter-in-law Ruby Cutshaw and granddaughter Sherry Redden

Iva O'Neal Cutshaw

Dear friends in Christ, you know the importance of this ministry and the weight of your responsibility in presenting Iva Cutshaw for ordination to the sacred priesthood...Is it your will that Iva be ordained a priest?

The Ordination of a Priest

"It is," declared an enthusiastic congregation in St. Paul's Church, Vernal, Utah, in August, 1987, when Iva Cutshaw stood before Bishop George E. Bates as the ordination service began. Iva Cutshaw had been "put forth" by her own congregation, chosen from among them for the sacred order of priesthood. This seventy-one-year-old grandmother is one of a number of priests ordered to a ministry of servanthood under the special provisions of Title III, Canon 11. Currently about twenty women and eighty men serve as Canon 11 priests in the Episcopal Church.

Essentially, hers is a ministry of obedience. She will continue to live in Vernal, where she has spent the last forty years, carrying out tasks assigned by the bishop. For the present, she has been assigned to take services at Holy Spirit mission in Randlett, three Sundays a month. The fourth Sunday, she holds services in Vernal while the rector, Gene Hutchins, goes to Randlett. (Another Canon 11 priest ordained with Cutshaw, Albert [Sonny] Beacham, has a similar assignment to St. Elizabeth's, Whiterocks.) The two churches outside Vernal are missions to the Ute Indians, small congregations that have met, intermittently, for many years. The Native American people to whom they minister are poor, still living on the arid land to which their ancestors were assigned a century ago and supported in part by royalties from reservation oil wells.

Those members of the tribes who have become Christian share a deep spirituality. "You take an Indian who is sincere, he is much more spiritual than a white man ever dares to be. They just have a quality deep within them, something that we can hardly fathom," Cutshaw explained. "I was the Selective Service coordinator for the whole county, and I have a good rapport with most of the Indians. And yet I also realize that they have their own ways. Things mean something a little different to them than they do to us, but they are very, very sincere and very spiritual."

Before he assigned Cutshaw to work with the Native Americans, Bishop Bates met with delegations from both parishes. When he asked how they would like to have Cutshaw and Beacham serving them, the Holy Spirit members said they had known the two for years and would have no objections at all. But the people at St. Elizabeth's were hesitant about having a woman priest. However, since services had been so intermittent there because of the lack of priests, they reluctantly accepted the plan. "I am really anxious to see what the association there will be," admitted Cutshaw. "I pray about it constantly. So far, it's been going real well. In fact, one Sunday, Sonny could not go to Whiterocks so six of those members came to my service at Holy Spirit. Evidently, I've been accepted as a priest, at least by some of that congregation."

The people at Holy Spirit are delighted to have a priest with them for regular services again. Sunday morning attendance has increased; five people have been baptized and Father Hutchins has begun a confirmation class. Under Cutshaw's leadership, a spirit of warmth has enveloped the congregation. "When we passed the peace, the people were reserved at first and shook hands," she said, "but now, you usually get a hug! It's naturally a very loving community, and they've opened the circle to include me." When she was asked to take the Eucharist to one of the parishioner's sisters who was in the hospital, she found eight people in the room waiting. "They all wanted to break bread with Priscilla," Cutshaw explained.

Harsh living conditions make the ministry difficult. On the high plateau area of the central Rockies, summers swelter with little shade from the sun's intense heat, while winters are long—with gale winds and driving blizzards. Cutshaw knows to keep a shovel, an extra blanket and emergency flares in her car as she drives the twenty miles to and from Randlett in the winter months.

The church is a small, frame, gothic structure, built when the Episcopal Church was first assigned the Ute ministry by the U.S. Bureau of Indian Affairs. A small trailer has been moved next door to serve as a parish house and Sunday school. "We resurrected the Sunday school when I came," explained Cutshaw in November, "and have been having about twelve or thirteen constant students. But the trailer has no heat and last week it got so cold that the water in the pipes froze. So I don't know yet what we will do about a place for Sunday school during the winter."

Cutshaw is deeply thankful that she can provide a steady ministry to the Ute Indians. As she explained, "The problem with the Episcopalians, according to my observations over the last forty years, is that the church would send a priest to Holy Spirit and he would just go gung-ho for awhile. Then he'd be withdrawn or transferred and it would be a long period of time before they had anyone to serve them again. And they would sort of scatter or go to other churches that would draw them. I feel real bad about what the church has done to the Indians, but hopefully it will get back on an even keel. Then, perhaps, they will raise up some of their own people as candidates for priesthood."

As a Canon 11 priest, Cutshaw did not go to seminary but rather participated in a two-year home study course, supervised by her rector. Though she has been ordained priest, the supervised learning continues. She has assisted at baptisms, weddings and funerals but has yet to do them on her own. She has begun to write her own sermons which are critiqued by Father Hutchins before she preaches them. When he is convinced that she is ready, she will be given a license to preach. "Some of the other priests were worried about us," she admitted, "but we have just had to make it clear that we were not here to take their place. That is not the idea of the program at all. We are to serve where there is a need. When we first began, the idea was for us to serve only within our home parish but then the bishop extended it to outlying parishes too."

When asked whether she would be paid by the diocese or the congregation she served, she replied, "Oh, there is no pay with this ministry, no pay at all. Our traveling expenses will be taken care of but that's it. We serve without compensation." Cutshaw has served St. Paul's Church that way for many years—as warden, vestry member, secretary, janitor. "She knew how to fix anything and everything," friend Cynthia Worthington explained. "She really took care of the church. She repaired screen doors and did the painting. She fixed the refrigerator when it went out and checked the furnace each year before it was time to start it up."

"I was in a prayer group with her and we all received a lot of strength from her," said Virginia Ashton, who has since moved to Salt Lake City. "She is a true friend. I don't know anyone who has been kinder to more people. They don't even have to be Episcopalians!"

For most of her life, Cutshaw has been involved in helping other people. She worked for years as the county Selective Service chairman and found a real ministry there to young men of draft age and their parents, particularly during the turbulent sixties. Then her husband discovered he had terminal cancer and she cared for him until his death. She herself had surgery for breast cancer. And she brought her mother to live with her when the older woman became too frail to live alone. Through this troubled period, the nagging sense of God's call grew steadily stronger.

"I guess I made a commitment years ago. My mother was with me and she was not in good health. One time I was cleaning the windows over at the church and was hit with a real bad spell. I went to the doctor down in Salt Lake and found it was my heart. I said to the Lord, 'If you will just let me keep my health so that I can take care of mother, so that she will not have to go to a nursing home, then I am with you for you to do what you want with me.' And from there on out one incident followed another—all of which seemed to be leading me to this path. I know that that really was a gift."

The seemingly constant confrontation with death drove Cutshaw to a quest for spiritual reality. "She has a very keen mind and an insatiable curiosity," said one friend. "She was always wondering why things weren't this way or that way. How come? why? what for? why not? seemed to be her favorite questions. She really and truly wanted to know the why and wherefore of everything. At first, she had no desire to be a priest; she thought it was just terrible that women would even think of being priests. But gradually she realized that that was what God was calling her to do."

"Now, I'm not smart in theology. I know that Jesus was born—as God's son. That he lived here on earth. That he died for our sins. That there is a Father, Son, and Holy Spirit—further than that I can't do what the seminarians can do," Cutshaw admitted. But what she can do is sit with people through their troubles—counseling, consoling, praying with them. She can witness to God's presence in a small Indian ranchhouse as family and friends gather to mourn the death of a loved one. She can establish a prayer network that connects the isolated and scattered members of her flock and nourishes and sustains them in time of need.

"Most people I know stand in awe of her and all the things

that she is able to do," said one parishioner. "People respect her and they turn to her. People not just from the town of Vernal but people she's met throughout her life. People in this diocese who, after a meeting, will seek her out and ask for her prayers. Her clear, unmistakable love of God and desire to serve Him really shows through. People in the parish respond to her. Sometimes, because they know her so well, they respond with frustration at her perfectionism, but mostly with a great deal of love."

Mary Chotard Doll

In all that you do, you are to nourish Christ's people from the riches of his grace, and strengthen them to glorify God in this life and in the life to come.

The Examination

"I know that I was called to be a part of that process," said Chotard Doll about her experience as one of the nominees for suffragan bishop of Washington. "I went to the interviews and the clergy conference there with the knowledge that I was bringing the gift of myself and nothing else except the Holy Spirit as people might see the Spirit through me. I was, therefore, as open and as vulnerable and as sharing as I knew how to be. I found that my doing so changed the nature of the interviewing process. I watched the other candidates move closer to openness and vulnerability. I watched the clergy of the diocese begin to believe that they could share the same spirit."

One of the first women to be nominated for bishop, Chotard Doll was clearly a viable candidate for the position. She had six years of experience as the rector of a major Cincinnati parish, and previous to ordination, had worked as an intelligence research analyst for the U.S. government—a significant credential to anyone who might be bishop in the nation's capital. She was known as an excellent preacher and tenacious pastor. Since her father had been bishop of Maryland, she knew well the pressures of episcopal life. In interviews she came across as an intelligent, thoughtful and gracious individual.

"I nominated Chotard Doll," said Verna Dozier, one of the church's leading lay theologians, "not because she was a woman but because I thought she was the best candidate. She had grown up in the house of a bishop so she knew what the office required. She was strong in the pastoral area. I believe that a man with those qualifications would have been elected."

Mary Chotard Doll

Though Chotard Doll was not chosen as bishop in the May, 1986, election, her acceptance by the clergy was indicated by the fact that she came within eight votes of receiving a majority of their votes on the fourth ballot. "For me, that was the great joy of the whole process," she said. "I believe that through my candidacy, the clergy of the Diocese of Washington moved past their preconceptions, and grew in their vision of the episcopate and how it might be exercised."

The process was difficult and painful for Doll. Naturally a rather private individual, she was uneasy at the excessive publicity. As the only woman nominated, she felt that unwarranted attention was focused upon her as a "token woman." Though supported by her husband, a classics professor who had assured her he was willing to move to Washington, she knew that their teenage son was upset by the possibility of dislocation. Most significant was the psychological strain; during the interviewing process, she moved from the belief that she would never be elected to a point where she felt that her election might be a real possibility. And then, as she listened to the balloting, she realized how many people simply refused to consider her qualifications because she was a woman.

Doll is rector of Calvary Church, a medium sized parish near the University of Cincinnati, with a membership of faculty, students and professionals. Worshiping in a building over a hundred years old, the congregation is quite traditional. In 1980 when they were searching for a rector, they probably would not even have considered a woman were it not for a diocesan policy that required all churches engaged in a search process to interview at least one woman. On the bishop's recommendation, the calling committee interviewed Doll and, after also visiting at St. George's Church in Dayton where she served as an intern, they unanimously recommended her as rector. "I was totally overwhelmed and greatly surprised," she admitted, "and both challenged and terrified at the prospect of being rector." Though she considered both reactions, the challenges won out and she accepted the position, becoming the first woman to serve as rector in Southern Ohio.

Her time is consumed primarily with administrative tasks, liturgical actions, relationships with various committees and councils and pastoral counseling. She has been dedicated to encouraging the people of the parish to take their own responsibility rather than expecting her to make all the decisions--a new model of leadership for Calvary and one that has taken time to implement. She has also sought to deepen the spiritual life of the congregation through quiet days and retreats and guided spiritual direction for individuals.

"She is terrific in pastoral care with the sick and aged," testifies former senior warden Kristian Berger. "She is a very caring person to all the parishioners." One parishioner, a clergyman's daughter who did not like the idea of women priests, has changed her mind because Doll "helped me feel at home at Calvary, as if I were part of the family."

What does Doll find most frustrating? "Trying to move the congregation from a very conservative liturgical tradition to a new understanding of the Eucharist—to enliven and improve the forms of celebrating the Eucharist. Episcopalians have always been able to sit back and be passive people present in the liturgy. It's hard for them to have a lively sense of God and the Holy Spirit living in them and moving through them. I stand in the pulpit and preach my heart out and long for these people to reach the point where they can accept the new life, to be the Easter people. I realize that my longing for people to know and experience the Holy Spirit in that way is something I can't give them—it's something they must experience for themselves."

"I might say she moves too quickly with innovative ideas," complained one vestry member, "particularly with changing the liturgy."

As rector, Doll has pushed for other changes as well. A parish outreach commission was established, pledging ten per cent of all income to work outside the parish. People have been encouraged to invest their time and talents—renovating urban housing, serving dinner in a downtown soup kitchen or tutoring illiterate immigrants from Appalachia.

Chotard Doll's personal life has also changed dramatically since she became Calvary's rector, for in 1984 she married Bernard Carl Fenik, a widower with two teenaged children. He was a parishioner whom she had counseled when his wife died of cancer.

Their marriage is unusual in many respects. Their hours of work are different. As a professor—he teaches Greek and Latin at the University of Cincinnati—he can be home most afternoons by three and has weekends free. She has heavy responsibilities on Sundays and many evening meetings and travels more often. So he handles the basic household tasks and does the laundry. Though they often cook together, he plans the meals and buys groceries.

Daughter Kirsten is away now at hotel management school in Germany, but for son Matthew, moving to the fishbowl life of a rectory has meant some adjustment. "I made it clear to him that I was not his mother—he remembers her quite clearly. But I am now working in the family structure as his parent—that is taking part in the understandings about curfews and driving and school-work—all those concerns that parents have. It's been a good relationship—he's very loving to me. He's an extroverted, outgoing person and frequently pops over to the church to see what's going on since he feels like that's his territory."

Matthew attends a Roman Catholic school and has enjoyed the notoriety there of having a mother who is a priest. "I think he's proud of it," she said. "He's written two themes about it, and offered me to his teachers as someone who could come to speak about the ordination of women."

Overall, her marriage and new family have made Doll's life as a priest much easier, she stressed. "Being married this late, I recognize the value and importance of family; I know I must take time to spend with my family and that time must be *quality time.* That's important to me! I am also aware of how blessed I am to have a husband who is as cooperative and supportive as mine is."

Having grown up in a rectory, Doll knew first hand the pressures on a clergy family. After she finished college and moved away from home, her church attendance lapsed. Working as a "spy" for the National Security Agency, she lived in the Washington area for seven years, then moved to Ohio where her fiance lived. It was the breakup of that love affair that brought her back to the church. "I felt that by trying to control everything myself, I had made a mess of my life, so I very consciously asked God to be present in my life and take charge. Things have never been the same since that moment."

Leaving her job in Columbus, she became parish administrator at St. Mark's Church there. While she enjoyed the work, increasingly she found herself involved in theological discussions about women and ministry. Finally, in the spring of 1975, she realized that she was really considering priesthood for herself. With the support of her rector, Edward C. Chalfant, and the parish, she entered Virginia Theological Seminary at the age of thirty-five. What was her parents' response to that move? "They literally said, 'We've been expecting that for some time.'"

Speaking of the ordination process, she said, "Everything moved with enormous smoothness for me; I'm quite blessed in that. By that time I had found a lot of self-assurance about who I was as a person. I knew what my gifts were and what my limitations were and was able to accept the fact that this really was a way to use them which was consonant with God's work in my life.''

What does she feel are the personal rewards in her work today? ''The relationship things: watching people grow, seeing people begin to heal, people who've been coming to the healing service here at Calvary for years for healing for body and spirit—to see them grow toward the wholeness that God intends for them to have. I find that being given the privilege of representing the Holy in any meeting—whether it be a group meeting or a hospital room or a classroom—is the thing that gives me life, that keeps me going in the midst of all the difficulties and not-quite-so-fulfilling things.''

How is her ministry different because she is a woman? ''It's a question of role models. My most important understanding came when I realized that my father and the person who served as my mentor were wonderful models but that I could not be like either one of them. Rather, I needed to rejoice in that fact and not feel bad about it and to begin to make my own decisions. I had to recognize that I had my own gifts that I must use—my own intelligence, my own instincts and my own faith. The sexual difference is positive in that sense. Once I came to grips with it and accepted it as a positive thing, I felt enormously freed.''

''As a woman, I bring to this task of priesthood the knowledge that I have the freedom in this society to be vulnerable, to be wrong, to be emotional and to put a lot of dependence on relationships. Now, many men have struggled to reach that same point but it is to women that our society gives permission for this kind of openness and vulnerability. Society allows women to be close to people—to be by them at the sick bed or at child birth or after a death—it frees us to be present to people in their faith experiences.''

''Another gift that women bring to the priesthood has to do with the image of God. When men and women stand together at the altar, it is only in our togetherness that we come near to imaging the wholeness of God. I have a male assistant—Charles

Brumbaugh—for the first time this year; and there is great joy for us both in celebrating the Eucharist together, one presiding but taking turns, for together we image God in the wholeness of male and female because that is the way we were created."

Doll is excited about her work at Calvary. This year her focus is to bring the parish to a deeper understanding of the meaning of stewardship—"what it really means to return to God a portion of all that has been given us." The work will begin with a vestry self-analysis, studying how well its stewardship represents the entire parish. "We are looking very hard at how the vestry can take responsibility for direction of the parish and then let the commissions carry out the various tasks." Helping others develop their own potential for leadership is one of Chotard Doll's greatest satisfactions.

Daphne Buchanan Grimes

For all who have died in the communion of your Church, and those whose faith is known to you alone, that, with all the saints, they may have rest in that place where there is no pain or grief, but life eternal, we pray to you, O Lord.

The Litany for Ordinations

Liturgical Emmaus

In the stillness, Lord,
When the bread is broken,
Broken, shared,
But none the less broken,
Nourishment, ours,
Through your pain of giving,
Pain in my heart
At my broken loving,
Be known to me, Lord,
In the breaking of bread.

Grimes, *Jerusalem Journal*

Daphne Grimes is a poet and an artist. She seeks, through carefully ordered words and line drawings, to explore the connection between surface reality and inner depth. Her sense of the depth and mystery of God is profound.

"Every leader must be a disciple at some times.... You must have a place where you can be sitting at the feet of someone else—where you can find refreshment and new vision." For Grimes, much of 1987 was an exploration of the dimensions of discipleship—an attempt to find strength and healing and joy as she followed the Lord's difficult path. Her Christian quest had spanned three decades and several continents, culminating finally in the admission that she was called to priesthood. Yet just before she

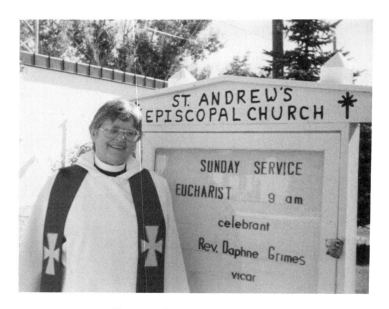

Daphne Buchanan Grimes

was to be ordained priest, her husband, Tommy, developed a brain tumor. He died within six months. Her first priestly acts were to consecrate a plot of land on their ranch as a cemetery and to hold Tommy's burial service.

"We'd had a very good, strong, close marriage. It was Tommy who had given me back myself when I was a pretty mixed up person. It was his trust and his love unconditionally granted to me that let me finally become myself rather than the lonely and afraid searcher I had been for so long. I didn't know what I was going to be able to do without him. All I knew was that the one thing he would have wanted was for me to move ahead. He was so glad that I had the priesthood I had been working so long for to look forward to."

Daphne spoke from the windswept plains of northeastern Wyoming where she serves as vicar of St. Andrew's Church, Meeteetse. Though the church building has stood in the ranch community for almost a century, the congregation has remained small—about twenty-five families and a number of single persons. For most of its history, St. Andrew's was served by occasional visits from clergy from other towns—chiefly Cody, thirty miles north. In 1979, Gail Baldwin became the first resident vicar. "Her work paved the way for me," Grimes explained, "because the people of Meeteetse had had such a good experience with one woman priest, they were exceedingly happy to receive another one."

Grimes' work includes the general round of weekly services, sacramental acts—baptisms, marriages, burials—and visiting her flock—who live on ranches scattered throughout a forty-mile area. The Old West is still very much alive in Meeteetse. Cowboy boots are standard dress—even for church. Strangers are welcomed, yet regarded with suspicion until they've proved themselves trustworthy. People are judged less by what they say than by what they do. The open spaces and long hours of solitary work have endowed the people themselves with a silence that is at once unassuming and profound.

Though one might suppose that women priests would be unwelcome in this cowboy world, Grimes has not found this to be true. Working also at the Chemical Dependency Center in Cody, she spends much of her time there counseling people who had turned to alcohol or drugs to combat their own loneliness and insecurity, and awakening them to their own hidden spirituality. "On very homely levels, these people are willing to open up to me *because* I am a woman."

The ministry to such small communities as Meeteetse is one area where women priests have been particularly effective. St. Andrew's is a congregation where present economic conditions make it difficult to support a full-time, resident priest. Grimes has been willing to work at a part-time salary in order to carry out her ministry to that congregation. The reality is that she is able to do this because of the financial security provided by her husband and the home she already owns. Many other women priests have been willing to work in such marginal situations for similar reasons. Not needing to depend on the church for their total support, some women have chosen to work fewer hours to minister to such small congregations. Others find themselves living in a certain area because of their husband's occupation and are willing to patch together several different positions in order to function as priests in that particular locality.

Moving to Wyoming was a symbolic homecoming for Daphne Grimes. She was born in Tulsa, Oklahoma, and raised in Houston, Texas, where her father worked as an exploration geologist. Graduating from high school just after World War II, she attended Wellesley College for two years, then returned to Texas where she received a bachelor of fine arts degree from the University of Houston. Moving to New York City, she took an M.A. in English and art history at Columbia University. Her interest in art led her to Europe where she spent the next five years studying and working, primarily in Rome and Florence. Later she returned and taught for two years at Rockland Country Day School in Nyack, New York.

Meanwhile her father had been sent to Tunisia to manage an oil exploration center. Joining her parents there, she was intrigued by the Moslem culture and stayed in Tunis for two years, teaching at the American Cooperative School. She met and married Thomas Edward Grimes, a geophysicist who worked for a Houston-based company. They lived four years in Libya, just outside of Tripoli in an area of small villas overlooking the Mediterranean.

Tommy's job brought him back to Houston as an executive in his company, where the Grimeses lived for over a year, until returning to Old Windsor, England, where Tommy headed his company's overseas exploration program for the next nine years. Although his work involved extensive travel, where he was frequently accompanied by Daphne, they also enjoyed English village life. Daphne particularly immersed herself in the local parish of Ss. Peter and Andrew. The vicar and his wife, Colin and Barbara Aspell, became intimate friends. At the recommendation of Canon Stephen Verney of St. George's Chapel, Windsor, she also enrolled at the Institute of Christian Studies, founded by Michael Marshall, who later became bishop of Woolwich, in London. On a more charismatic front, the Community of Celebration (known to Americans as the Fisherfolk) had a house nearby, and Daphne became deeply involved in the life of that group.

In 1978, the Grimeses moved back to the United States. "We had seen so many expatriates who returned to America upon retiring and found they were just too old to establish for themselves a real home there. We didn't want that to happen to us. So Tommy left his job with the geophysical company and we moved to Cody where we built a house on the ranch where my parents had lived. When he was not traveling Tommy worked with the ranch's manager. We joined Christ Church, Cody, and dedicated ourselves to rediscovering the wild West."

Shortly after moving to Wyoming, a casual conversation with her rector, Patterson Keller, finally articulated Daphne's call. She had complained about the lack of Eucharist celebrations since he had been on vacation and there were no nearby priests. "What about you," asked Keller, "have you ever thought of going into the ministry?"

"When I answered yes, I surprised myself," admitted Grimes, "because I had never allowed myself to consider that possibility, But suddenly everything was clear. I heard God's call and felt myself answering, 'I will go as far as you want me to go.'"

From that moment, she began a series of steps to test that call. She wrote to the bishop of Wyoming, Bob Jones, who wasn't sure what to do with someone who had been absent from the American church for twenty years. Urging her to involve herself in parish activities, he later appointed her chairman of the diocesan stewardship commission. "That was a vantage point from which to learn a great deal about the Episcopal Church very quickly," she said. After serving as a mentor for the Education for Ministry program, she completed the diocesan diaconal training program and enrolled in a course in clinical pastoral education at St. Luke's Hospital in Houston. Back in Cody, she was ordained deacon and worked for a year in that capacity at Christ Church.

Each stage strengthened her perception that she was called to priesthood. Finally, the bishop agreed to allow her to enter the Episcopal Theological Seminary of the Southwest in Austin, Texas. Because of her extensive course work abroad, she was able to complete a master of arts in religion degree in just over a year. "I could not have done that without Tommy's support. Being in Austin so far away from him was terribly lonely. He came down when he could and never complained about my being away."

By the end of 1985, the Grimeses' life seemed to be prospering. They were back together on the ranch with Tommy's recent sojourns in China and Australia over. Daphne was serving as deacon at Christ Church and as chaplain at the Chemical Dependency Center. The last steps of her candidacy for priesthood were under way.

Just as all the pieces of their lives seemed in order, the harmony was shattered with the discovery that Tommy had an incurable brain tumor. The next six months were a desperate attempt to at least mitigate the effects of the tumor—trips to Houston for radiation treatment, rearranging the Wyoming house to make Tommy more comfortable, trying to speak the necessary words while speech was still possible. And all the while they continued plans for Daphne's ordination because Tommy wanted to be part of that service. Though he died on October 22, she went ahead with the November 1 ordination because she knew he would have it so.

Then the grief set in. She felt empty, void, enervated. Her pain was heightened by the fact that her brother's wife had died just two days after Tommy and there were complex family matters to settle. After weeks of a sort of detachment from life, she sought healing by retracing the steps of their life together. She returned to England, visiting friends there and spending some time in retreat at the Community of St. Andrew in London, sharing with many of the member deaconesses their joy at the Church of England's recent decision to allow them to be ordered as deacons. Then she went on to St. George's College in Jerusalem where a structured study course in bible and worship, culminating in the celebration of Easter week, provided both intellectual and emotional sustenance. Her pilgrimage ended at Holy Savior Priory in South Carolina where she was able to work with a counselor. "For the first time, I was able to get in touch with a lot of my own anger and grief. I made a quantum leap in coming back to being a functional person again."

On her return to Wyoming in May, 1987, she was installed as vicar of St. Andrew's Church, Meeteetse. "The position was a real blessing from God—St. Andrew's is such an exciting place to be with this new ministry ahead of me," she declared. For the present, she is concentrating her energy on her work with the congregation. "The breadth and the openness of that small rural community just amazes me," she said. "To see their receptivity, their love, their concern for each other is astounding. I've never lived among a community this small before. Meeteetse is only 512 people. The potential and the growth and the enthusiasm and the care in this small community makes me realize how much the church, if it is to be truly a body, has to be in a place where we can be intimate enough to really be in touch with each other. We have to keep things at the human dimension in order to enable the full God-expression of ourselves to live itself out in love with each other."

A persistent dream, however, lurks at the back of her mind—the possibility of establishing a retreat center at her ranch in the Wyoming mountains. "I am not ready to talk about that yet," she cautioned. "I am only too aware of what an enormous task that would be. And yet, I know how my spirit has been fed at such places around the world. My tasks at the moment are to wait and pray and learn as much as I can about such centers. I'll leave the rest to God."

Carmen Bruni Guerrero

For the mission of the Church, that in faithful witness it may preach the Gospel to the ends of the earth, we pray to you, O Lord.

The Litany for Ordinations

"When I first came to Santa Fe Mission, the whole place was locked up. There were burglar bars everywhere; everything had locks on it. The day was cold, in the middle of winter, and it was a real dead-looking place. But the people saw my car outside, and at least ten families came by, either to inquire what I was doing there or to look for help. Almost everybody that came had a need of some sort. And all I had to give them was grapefruit."

Carmen Bruni Guerrero's first day at the mission, located in a predominantly Hispanic section of San Antonio, Texas, was less discouraging than the second day, when she returned to find a long line of people waiting for grapefruit. No one had told her there was a weekly distribution of the fruit at this location. "I assumed that they were there because I had given grapefruit out the day before, and the word was out and now what was I going to do? Where in the world was I going to get it from?" Fortunately, the trucks arrived with cases of grapefruit and distribution proceeded. But Guerrero could not let it stop there.

"I began to think, there's something missing here; this many people would gather together to pick up grapefruit and yet it was a good, good Sunday morning when they had fifteen people in church. Something's not right, something's not connecting here. So I decided that the next Wednesday when they came, I would turn on the heat, get some cookies, make some coffee and invite the people to wait inside the parish hall where it would be warm. I did that. And when they came in, we began to talk. I found that there was hardly anybody who had not, in one way or another, been touched by some kind of ministry from this church.

Carmen Bruni Guerrero   Photo: Houston Chronicle

And I said, 'If you could see this place come alive again, what would you like to see happen?'''

That was the beginning of a resurrection story. Santa Fe Mission has come alive. In March, 1987, Guerrero was appointed vicar of the church. She listened to the people who said they would like to meet for Bible study—before the grapefruit arrived. And when the harvest season was over, the people continued to come. They added a potluck luncheon on Wednesdays; those who had food shared with those who had none. "I had the strong idea that Bible study was a way to begin to feed people spiritually and that would take care of feeding people into the church on Sunday," said Guerrero. And so it did.

Sunday morning congregations increased in size. A second Bible study was set up on Tuesday nights. A young woman who played the guitar volunteered her services and they added music to the evening's program. When she went off to school, men came forward to play. "We Latin people are very much a people of fiesta, of celebration. We love the music," Guerrero explained.

The vitality of the worship services and the Bible study propelled parishioners into other activities. They have established literacy classes to teach English to the Hispanic residents—a program for which the local school district now provides a full-time certified teacher. There is a weekly sewing and handicraft class. The mission serves as a center for the legalization of undocumented people through the U.S. government amnesty program. A food bank and clothing depot is available for those in need.

The local people are also supporting the program financially. Because of the poverty of the surrounding neighborhood, it was estimated that the mission could probably provide about $8,000 for its own program. "But in the first nine months, we've already brought in $22,000," said Guerrero proudly. "We have received at least $15,000 of in-kind help because the people don't always have the actual cash but they are extremely willing to help. It was just a matter of people beginning to believe that they are part of the church—that they are members of something greater than themselves."

Guerrero's leadership style has been an important factor in the change. She's worked hard to get people involved in the parish, setting up a men's group and a women's group, an acolyte's guild and a choir. Vestry members are encouraged to take leadership and make decisions for the parish; committees on finances and Christian education work to carry out those decisions. "I believe in delegation of duties; I'm not going to do it all by myself," she said, adding, "When I first came, having a woman priest was a novelty. But then they saw how serious I am about the Lord Jesus Christ, about the Spirit of God, about working together, about the value of who we are because we are created in the image of God. I'm not playing around with that; I would stake my life on it. That seems to empower my people to believe it too. And we sort of grow into it together, rather than just one person telling them—it's a community effort."

"I think one of the most frustrating things for me is that there is a verbal commitment to Hispanic ministry in this diocese, but very few finances. I know that in the United States, the things that we really back are not the things we talk about but those that we put our money in. And in this diocese, our financial commitment has not yet begun to match our verbal commitment. But what I hope to accomplish at Santa Fe Church is that the people will begin to believe in themselves and will get rid of that mentality that says, 'If the diocese won't help us, then we'll never make it.' Because they *can* make it for themselves," Guerrero asserted.

Guerrero, herself, is an important role model for her flock. She grew up in one of the government housing projects in San Antonio, daughter of a Roman Catholic father and protestant mother of Mexican ancestry. Since her family had limited financial resources, church became for her a way out of the project. Many churches provided buses for Sunday services and Guerrero literally took whatever bus came by, simply as a means of entertainment, a trip into an expanded world. She eventually joined the Evangelical Free Church and was actively involved in many of its programs. She married and raised her son in that faith.

"Then ten years ago I got a divorce," she said, "and the way they see things theologically left no room for me in that church. If they accepted me, then they were faced with condoning divorce. If they didn't accept me, then they were repudiating the forgiveness they preached. And that was a very painful time for me because that was the only church home I knew."

She met some Episcopalians who were involved in a Faith Alive program and they invited her to a Bible study group at Christ Church, San Antonio. "I knew a little bit more about the Bible than the people in that group knew and they knew a whole lot more about the love of God than I was experiencing at the time. The connection was just perfect! I remember saying that if I had known the Episcopal Church was that alive, I would have been there years ago; but I was assured by some people that it wasn't that way everywhere," she admitted. She and her son were both confirmed and she began to invest her energy in the Faith Alive movement.

At that point, Guerrero was coordinating guidance programs for inner city black and Mexican youths in trouble with the law. Becoming convinced that the family was the key to helping such young people, she had returned to college for a master's degree in clinical counseling, specializing in family therapy. But just as she finished that program, she felt a distinct call to go to seminary for further theological education.

Because she was so new in the Episcopal Church, the bishop would not accept her as a candidate for ordination. So she agreed to wait a year, and found a position as the protestant chaplain at Santa Rosa Medical Center, a Roman Catholic hospital. "I felt I should have paid them for all that they taught me," she said.

A year later, in the fall of 1981, Carmen Guerrero entered the School of Theology at the University of the South. "I chose Sewanee because I wanted an experience out of my culture; I didn't want to be put in a box for, and only for, Hispanic ministry. Though Hispanic ministry is very much what I am about, there is a whole lot more to me than just that. And surely Sewanee did turn out to be a cultural experience that was totally different from anything that I have ever lived!"

Just at the end of her last year at Sewanee, Bishop Leopold Frade of Honduras appeared on campus to explore the possibility of establishing a theological education program by extension in his diocese to train Honduran priests. He met Guerrero and asked her to be its director. "The minute we got through talking, I knew that was it. That was where God was calling me and that's what I needed to do. It was so right that I was even afraid to believe it because it just mattered so much to me at the time," she said.

So after graduating from Sewanee and being ordained deacon in San Antonio, Carmen Guerrero went to Honduras to organize a theological training program. Honduras had only nine clergy in the entire diocese when she arrived; twenty-three students (men and women) were in various phases of the training when she left. Bishop Frade ordained her to the priesthood for the Diocese of West Texas and gave her charge of two small rural congregations.

One of those churches, St. Paul the Apostle, was in Calpules, a village the people had established on property owned by absentee landlords. One day she arrived to find soldiers had been there to drive the people off the land. "They had destroyed all the homes—just axed everything away. They had waited until the men had gone to work so that the women were alone. They killed the chickens; they killed the goats and hung them on the fence. The first thing that came into my mind was that I needed a lawyer and I needed the press." She couldn't find a lawyer who dared oppose the landlords but she did at least get some reporters to come to document the damage.

What she remembered most about the incident was the faith of the people. "Those people taught me a whole, whole lot about the cross. One of the things that kept going through my mind was 'How am I going to convince these people that they are not abandoned, that God is in their midst?' And the truth is, they already *knew* it. I asked them if they still wanted to have the Eucharist, and it had never occurred to them not to do that." Though the soldiers came back midway through the service, the people went right on with the worship, one soldier even joining them for communion. After she left, however, the families were driven from the land—to start again in another locale. Facing the complexity of the relationship between faith and such political realities was a bitter but terribly important learning process for Guerrero in Honduras.

When her two-year term was up, Guerrero reluctantly returned to the United States. "I went to Sewanee, to St. Mary's Convent, and spent a month there, literally grieving. I had learned a lot about me and my value there. It was the first time in my life that I had been in an environment where being an educated Hispanic person was not the exception. It was a powerful experience for me."

Since her return to San Antonio, she has continued her association with the national Volunteers for Mission program by becoming the coordinator of training for those interested in Hispanic ministry. Students are put through an intensive, ten-day orientation in Hispanic culture and mission theology, after which some of them are placed directly in overseas or domestic assignments and others remain in San Antonio to work on specific vocational or language skills. Through retreats and workshops in areas such as spirituality, prayer, time management, theology and biblical studies, Guerrero pushes the volunteers to understand the connection between their own faith and their actions and to define the basic cultural assumptions on which those actions are based.

Being coordinator of the volunteers program and vicar of Santa Fe Church are each half-time positions in which Guerrero invests far more than half of her time and energy. She works very hard. Since her son is now in college, her life has become quite centered in her work. "The priesthood puts heavy responsibilities on us— the needs of the people seem to be so great. And yet, I guess that's why we become priests, because we are initially helpers of people. It's rewarding, but it can also totally wipe you out if you are not careful to pastor yourself. I sometimes think that the men have it easier because they have someone at home who is taking care of them. As a single woman, I find that nobody's going to do my laundry or cook my meals! I get off work and still have to come home to do all those things."

She believes, though, that the rewards are worth the effort. "The greatest reward is giving people a sense of their own worth— knowing that I have contributed to their freedom, to their independence, to their believing that they are worthwhile human beings. Sharing the gospel and then following through by way of the sacraments—nurturing them into baptism through reconciliation, serving them at the Lord's table, uniting them in marriage, teaching them—the giving of those kinds of things is personally very rewarding to me. But it's also rewarding to receive. And I receive a lot from people—a lot of affirmation, a lot of being taken care of. I know that I am loved. I know that I am upheld in prayer and esteem—that's very rewarding to me. I have someone to give to and someone is giving to me."

Denise Lee Haines

For those in positions of public trust, that they may serve justice and promote the dignity and freedom of every person, we pray to you, O Lord.

The Litany for Ordinations

Located in one of the most densely populated areas in the United States, the Diocese of Newark is a microcosm of both the problems and the opportunities of urban America. Geographically, the diocese covers the northern third of New Jersey, with a majority of its parishes located in the urban megalopolis stretching from Bayonne north along the Hudson River opposite New York City, encompassing such cities as Jersey City, Hoboken, Paterson, Montclair, the Oranges, and Newark. Historically, the area's economic strength was based on its port facilities; even today extensive equipment for containerized shipping makes the Port of Newark one of the world's major terminals.

The conjunction of that port, several major railway lines, storage facilities for oil and natural gas, and a wide range of industrial plants produces a continuing demand for labor—a demand that is met by immigrants from many lands and by migrants from other parts of the United States. Moving into the older housing surrounding the center city, these people make up a community characterized by ethnic and racial diversity and dissociation from native cultures. Many of the people of this area are poor, living at bare subsistence levels. Housing is crowded, unemployment is high. The central cities struggle, with shrinking tax bases, to provide adequate schools, police and fire protection, health care and recreational and transportation facilities. In some areas, however, a growing prosperity has begun to change the neighborhood economy, bringing wealthy and middle income professionals back into the city. Urban Episcopalians number among the very rich as well as the poor.

Coordinating the ministry of the Episcopal Church to this

Denise Lee Haines

metropolitan strip is Denise Haines. As archdeacon for missions and urban ministry in the Diocese of Newark, her key responsibility is working with forty-five urban congregations, providing assistance for specific local problems as well as helping to shape a diocesan strategy for urban work. She also chairs the eighteen-member Department of Missions which oversees those congregations aided by the diocese, trying desperately to stretch its $500,000 budget to provide new programs and also keep pace with necessary upkeep and renovation of buildings—many built in the last century.

How does one woman manage to coordinate such a vast and varied constituency? An excellent administrator, Haines begins with a clear sense of her own position and the direction toward which she thinks the diocese ought to aim. "If we are going to do anything to change the outworn structures of our society to meet the human needs that are overwhelming us, there has to be a carefully set out and worked out plan," she explained. "Scheduling is very important. You have to allow a certain amount of time in your week to take initiative and not just be in a reacting mode."

Haines works simultaneously with an immediate schedule and a more far-reaching one, taking care to let the larger vision inform each day's activities. Since the focus on urban ministry has just been added to her job description, her most immediate goal is to work with the urban clergy. "We have some extraordinary clergy—men and women—in our urban congregations. By getting them together, giving them the opportunity to share with each other and to focus on strategies for urban ministry, we can begin to develop strong networks where people can accomplish things together." Building on the trust developed among the clergy, lay people will be added to the strategy sessions. "Eventually we hope to move into more ecumenical structures but we must strengthen our own base first."

When asked where such strategy might lead, she answered, "It appears fairly clear to me that today the energy in this part of the world—both within the church and outside of it—is focused on housing. In many of our cities, Episcopal churches have extensive physical plants that might be converted to multi-use facilities to meet the needs of a given neighborhood. We are long past the point where we can afford the luxury of maintaining a building that is used only three hours each week on Sunday morning. We also, as an hierarchical church, can develop the kind of resources necessary to develop workable housing projects." She is currently studying a plan that would provide mixed-income rental units around an atrium and gathering room—an architecture that mirrors the church's commitment to building community.

Urban strategy within the Diocese of Newark will depend not only on the needs of the inner city but also on the resources available in the wealthy suburban parishes on the western edge of the metropolitan area. Here, tree-lined streets and large single family homes from which commuters leave each morning for the daily bus or train ride into Manhattan or Newark isolate church members from the harsh realities of the more crowded areas. Denise knows this world well. Less than twenty years ago, she was a suburban housewife, married to Richard Haines whose business brought them to Summit, New Jersey. With their two sons and a daughter, they worked at church and volunteer activities. However, in the late sixties the various social movements—peace, civil rights, feminist—produced in Denise a spiritual restlessness which was amplified by the sudden death of both her parents a few months apart. In the chaos of her personal life, she turned to Calvary Church as an important place of stability. She enrolled in adult classes taught by an extraordinary teacher, the Reverend Robert Morris. He recognized her intellectual ability and, as she testifies, "really encouraged my mind."

"His classes whetted my appetite, convinced me that there was more that I wanted to know about theology, Bible, the world that really mattered—and I began to explore the possibility of going to seminary," she said. "Deciding to go to General Seminary was the first independent decision I had ever made. I had gone to college because my parents thought I ought to go—even majored in music (with an education minor) because my father thought that was a suitable major for a woman. I'd moved almost imperceptibly from the role of dutiful daughter to that of dutiful wife, following my husband's career moves from Delaware, to Tennessee, to New Jersey. But I had inherited some money from my parents and could afford, not only the tuition but also a very fine day-care program for Elizabeth, who was three years old the day I entered General."

Beginning in the fall of 1974, she commuted daily to the

seminary in New York, which at that time allowed women to enroll in the master of divinity program without the "priestly formation" requirements. Though she had not intended to seek ordination, other students and faculty members encouraged her to do so and eventually she applied for candidacy from the Diocese of Newark. The process went very smoothly. "I was ordained (deacon) eleven months after my initial visit with the bishop," she said. "I doubt that could happen again. I just came along before they really knew what to do with women candidates."

One of the seminary's degree requirements was a course in clinical pastoral education which she was able to take at Overlook Hospital in Summit, just three blocks from her home. "I was fortunate throughout this process to have a number of people enter my life who acted as mentors—who provided an imagination for what I might become. Bob Morris envisioned me as an intellectual; some of my seminary professors envisioned me as a priest; my supervisor at Overlook envisioned me as a hospital chaplain—even a clinical pastoral education supervisor. Though in a sense I feel these initiatives came from outside of me, I was able to live into the role models provided."

Doing just that, after seminary she entered a training program to become a certified chaplain supervisor at Allentown State Hospital in Pennsylvania, commuting daily sixty-five miles each way from Summit. After finishing the course in just over two years, she resigned from the Allentown chaplaincy, because, in her words, "I was exhausted! The emotional and intellectual demands of the training program and chaplaincy work combined with my family responsibilities and the long commute wore me out. I knew I needed a lighter assignment."

By this time she had been ordained priest, so she took a part-time position as assistant to the Reverend Walter Bell in nearby Chatham, New Jersey. St. Paul's Church was a rather preppy, well-to-do congregation of over six hundred members and Denise found herself returning to a familiar pattern of suburban church life. But just six weeks after she arrived, Bell resigned and she found herself in charge of the entire congregation while they searched for a new rector. Though she submitted her resignation when the new rector, John Branson, was finally called, he asked her to stay on as his assistant.

"It was an ideal situation. We just hit it off. He didn't like to do some of the things I liked to do and vice versa. I did take some intentional actions to establish the fact that I was no longer in charge. I cut my working time back to ten hours a week (then gradually assumed more hours). When people came to me with problems, unless I had already been working with them on those particular problems, I sent them to John." Though she loved the people with whom she worked, she gradually realized that she'd never really aspired to parish work. Feeling she would like to return to being a chaplain, she told the rector that she would resign as soon as he could find another assistant.

There were problems, too, in her family life in Summit. By the time she left St. Paul's, she and her husband had decided they could no longer continue their marriage. Suddenly confronted with the economic necessity of supporting herself, she turned to Bishop John Spong, who had just lost his archdeacon and needed administrative assistance. He offered her a part-time position on the diocesan staff. She countered with the proposition that she assume the archdeacon's position on a trial basis, and they finally agreed that she should take the office on a one-year contract, subject to renewal. "We didn't know whether this would work," she admitted. "I had absolutely no background or experience to lead either of us to believe I could do this job." But within three months, Haines' gift for administration and her ability to work effectively within difficult situations had earned the respect of both the bishop and the diocese.

Haines has served now as archdeacon since 1983. She continues to find a great deal of satisfaction in a position she finds exciting and challenging. The boundaries of her job have shifted; initially she also served as diocesan deployment officer, interviewing potential candidates and training search committees in the selection process. This responsibility has now been given to someone else in order to allow Haines to concentrate on urban ministry, an area she finds far too few seminaries and dioceses take seriously. To counter this problem, she sparked the development of an urban internship program—a nine-month course in urban ministry for seminarians, priests or qualified laity. Three interns have just completed the course, each working in a different parish under the rector's supervision but also meeting together and with diocesan agencies to gain an understanding of resources for urban change. On the basis of learnings from this pilot year, the program will be revised and strengthened and integrated as a strategy.

Haines is encouraged about the acceptance of women priests in the Diocese of Newark. Nineteen women priests serve in the diocese—four of them in the urban churches with which she works. "I do have the sense that some significant breakthroughs have occurred in this diocese since I took the position. My very visible presence as a woman in command has helped people imagine what it would be like to have a woman in charge of their congregations. Certainly, it has helped a great many people to imagine what it would be like to have a woman as a bishop. I suspect that my particular contribution has been in the enfleshment of an idea."

"The majority of able priests and lay people in the diocese think Denise does a superb job," testified Scott Kallstrom, vicar of Grace Church, Van Vorst. "She is an extremely able administrator—articulate and very intelligent. But there are those who fear her, partly because of her role of archdeacon. She is very demanding, which sometimes alienates others. She works too hard—which can be perceived as a threat."

Haines said, "The most difficult problems I wrestle with have nothing to do with my being a priest. They are human problems and can be found repeatedly in the great literature of the world. But the rewards of my priesthood are significant. There are the rewards of recognition, belonging, appreciation, self-actualization—those higher needs that Abraham Maslov lists as part of human development. There is enormous satisfaction in having a job where my deepest values as a human being are given expression. The job itself and the work that I do, the people I work with, also inform my values and expand them. I am able to contribute to my world in a way that simply was not possible when my life was completely circumscribed by domesticity."

Photo: Laurisa Baranyk

Marsue Harris

You are to preach, to declare God's forgiveness to penitent sinners, to pronounce God's blessing, to share in the administration of Holy Baptism and in the celebration of the mysteries of Christ's Body and Blood, and to perform the other ministrations entrusted to you.

The Examination

"Hope comes hard in prison. There are many men and women who 'do life on the installment plan.' There are few miracle stories to tell, and all too often, disappointing, if not violent, failures.

99

Maintaining the possibility of hope for a new life in or out of prison is the most challenging part of my work," explained Marsue Harris, protestant chaplain of the Rhode Island Adult Correctional Institutions.

For over fifteen years, Marsue Harris has worked in prisons—first in California as executive director of Friends Outside and now as the protestant chaplain in the huge Rhode Island prison complex which houses 1,200 men and 60 women. A small, lovely woman with curly brown hair, she would scarcely match one's image of a prison official. Yet when she speaks of her work within that institution, one immediately senses the dedication that has made her popular with inmates and officials alike. In the *San Quentin News,* prisoner Abdul Na'im Bismillah described her as "a very warm person, with a consoling voice who displays that rare human character of compassion." He added, "I thought it was significant to note that throughout the entire interview, she never once referred to any of the men she seeks to help as convicts; instead she chose to call everyone men."

Sponsored by the Rhode Island Council of Churches, Harris is the only protestant chaplain within the system—a complex of several facilities. She holds weekly protestant worship services and Bible study sessions and distributes Bibles and other spiritual reading materials. She officiates at marriages, baptisms and burials of staff and their families as well as for released inmates. She does individual and family counseling, prerelease assistance and meets with parolees when they return "to the street." She teaches a class at the Training Academy for new officers. Several of her counselees continue to call her for advice years after their release from prison.

Of particular significance has been her witness to the larger community about prisons and prisoners. She takes church groups through the prison and speaks through radio, television, church and service organizations about the penal system. She has organized and administers a team of thirty volunteers who share the work within and without the prison. "I work for change which will protect the public safety yet provide treatment programs which I pray will heal instead of punish offenders. The criminal justice system is slow and resistant to change, one of those 'principalities and powers' that William Stringfellow wrote so eloquently about," she explained.

Harris is also serving as the interim rector of St. Peter's by the Sea, a small parish in Narragansett. Though the town has been primarily a summer vacation community, it is in the process of becoming a year-round suburban and professional community. Along with providing a Sunday Eucharist and assisting the laity in their program planning, Harris sees her chief function there to "encourage the discussion of issues in the parish which will affect the selection and success of their relationship with a new priest."

Though her original understanding with the parish was that she would work one day a week and hold Sunday services, she has found herself spending many more hours there. That, plus the full-time job at the prison has proved to be too exhausting and she has asked the bishop to find another interim pastor who can devote more time to the parish. Why did she take on the parish work? "I love parish work. Having that different perspective is important to me. I think one of the reasons that I don't burn out in the prison work is that I do parish ministry also. And the reverse is true also—the prison provides a different perspective to parish work."

The road to priesthood was a rocky one for Harris. As a housewife with husband and two children living in the Salinas Valley in California, Harris had become an Episcopalian and started to work with Friends Outside at Soledad Prison. One day, when she complained to her rector, George N. Hunt, about the lack of spiritual help inside the prison, he challenged her to think about providing that help. "She voiced the usual excuses," Hunt recalled, "kids, a husband, the expense, the time involved. I told her, 'If it's important, you'll find a way to deal with all those issues.'"

Shortly thereafter, her marriage broke up leaving Marsue to support herself and children Laurisa and Nicholas. With great trepidation, she sold her home, moved to a public housing complex, took a job and entered the Church Divinity School of the Pacific as a part-time student. "My children would probably say they never want to live in public housing again. On the other hand, they spent seven years in a racially integrated neighborhood with its ups and downs, and were also able to articulate to their school friends what it meant not to have everything," she said, proud of the maturity the children found as they supported her call.

After finishing seminary, she was ordained priest in 1981 and assisted the rector of St. Stephen's Church in Belvedere, California, a wealthy suburban community. Even in that position, though, she continued her association with the penal system, serving on the Marin County Adult Criminal Justice Commission and the advisory board to San Quentin's house for inmates' families.

While she was in seminary, her former rector, George Hunt, had been elected bishop of Rhode Island. Though he knew that the Council of Churches there was looking for a prison chaplain, Hunt did not propose her name because he was convinced a woman had no business in a place as tough as the Adult Correctional Institutions. However, after the first two nominees for the job turned it down, "I rethought it and decided God was trying to tell us something," Hunt said. Harris flew from California, interviewed, and was offered the position. After hesitating and some soul-searching she accepted and made the long move with her family from the Pacific to the Atlantic coast.

"Through her prison work, she's done more to advance the cause of women's ordination than any other person in this diocese," Hunt proclaimed. "One of her most attractive qualities is that she's not afraid to take high risks, bite off more than she can chew. I guess it's as much a testimony to faith as to anything. She's saying, 'If God is in charge of my life, I have nothing to lose.'" A friend, Sandol Stoddard (now living in Hawaii) echoes that praise. "Marsue led me through an experience of personal loss in a way I will never forget. She is firmly grounded in her beliefs and does not hesitate to speak up for them or to live by them."

One person who was not comfortable with the idea of ordained women was Robin Porter, then junior warden at St. Ann's Mission on Block Island. When he heard that a woman priest was taking services there, he initially declined to be present. "Our senior warden persuaded me to attend services that Sunday, claiming this woman priest was someone special. She was right. Marsue preached with inspiration and humor. She challenged her listeners and shared something of herself. Within the hour, I discovered I had become a convert to the idea of women priests," he said. "It took me a little longer, but I also had the good sense to ask Marsue to become my wife. I am doubly blessed, you might say."

Though Marsue had feared that marriage would drain the energy she needed for ministry or that her self would be lost in the relationship, she found in marrying Robin that she had no need for such fears. "Robin supports me completely by enjoying and helping in the parish, by participating in household chores, by holding me day and night when the burden of prison and parish get the best of me for a moment, and by reflecting with me about how all this manifests itself in me. He enhances and enlarges my ability to minister."

Robin is an architect interested in historic preservation. They live in an 18th century home which they are restoring slowly. Son Nicholas, a high school senior, lives with them, while daughter, Laurisa, and Robin's four grown children are in and out of the house as vacations and work schedules permit.

What frustrates Harris the most about prison work? "I guess it's the repetition, the lack of change in lives. We see people who go through their whole lives without a lot of significant change. Some of them desperately want to be healed of their compulsions and addictions and they aren't being healed. And I see people who have very limited ability to cope with life—no education, social skills—you turn them loose in the world and they just can't survive. So you question, sometimes, the way God's world is made. Why do certain things happen to some people? Why are they not able to change? Keeping hope when so much seems hopeless, that's the most difficult thing I do," she admitted.

And yet, she's determined to do what she can to make life better for the inmates. She works hard to involve community members in caring ways. She is working with a Roman Catholic group that hopes to be able to establish a half-way house for those recently released. (Rhode Island has no half-way houses.)

She had raised some money for a similar facility two years ago when she thought she had someone who was willing to donate a house, but he withdrew the offer and, she said, "I just did not have the time to do it all myself."

Again and again, as she speaks to local churches or leads tours of the prison, she repeats her firm conclusion, "Prisons don't work. Punishment does not work. Virtually everybody who goes into prison comes back out. It's a misguided notion to think that once we lock people up, we're safe. Those same people will come back out and unless they get treatment and help, they will be worse threats to the community when they come out."

What sustains her as she continues this difficult work? "The first time I celebrated the Eucharist, I knew this was why I was born," she said. "I never know if I'm making a difference, but what keeps me here is the sense that I'm in the right place. I have no illusions that I'm changing the system; I just hope that the people I work with can have new dreams about their lives."

Victoria Hatch with Mel and Blanche Rhodes

Nancy Hatch Wittig and Victoria Theresa Hatch

For all who fear God and believe in you, Lord Christ, that our divisions may cease and that all may be one as you and the Father are one, we pray to you, O Lord.

The Litany for Ordinations.

"Wherever we lived in the United States or overseas, we always found an Episcopal Church. I was confirmed in Japan by the Presiding Bishop of the Nippon Sei Ko Kai, having taken comfirmation classes in Yokohama, an hour long bus ride from the naval base," explained Victoria Hatch. "In Munich, Germany, I taught Sunday school for the English-speaking congregation of St. Willibrord's Church. In Virginia, my father was superintendent of the Sunday school and my mother a member of the altar guild and the Episcopal Church Women."

Victoria and Nancy Hatch grew up in a family in which the Episcopal Church provided stability and definition in a world marked by dislocation and upheaval. Daughters of a career naval officer, they lived at several bases during the years just after World War II. "Living in Italy, Germany, England, and Japan, I had seen a church that went across national boundaries and denominational lines," Nancy said. "That simple understanding of the universality of the faith has sustained me and moved me into actions of personal and corporate boldness that I might never have attempted otherwise."

One such action was her decision to be one of the eleven women ordained in Philadelphia in 1974. By that time, she had received her master of divinity degree from Virginia Theological Seminary and had passed the national canonical examinations. Ordained deacon in September, 1973, she had worked as assistant at All Saints' Church, Millington, New Jersey.

"I read Mary Daly's *Beyond God the Father* in the summer of 1974. That book empowered me; it made me literally get up from the comfortable, safe, quiet country couch where I had been reading and say, 'Now I know what I am supposed to do. It is time for the church to move and to be changed, and if there is any way that I can have a part of it, that is what my responsibility is.' It was that clear, that firm, that definite," she said.

She told her bishop, George Rath of the Diocese of Newark, that she had agreed to be among the ordinands in Philadelphia and asked him to join the other ordaining bishops. Though he refused that request, he did not prohibit her presence at Philadelphia. For the women involved, the ordination held mystery and awe and a profound sense of God's grace. For Nancy, it was a joyous occasion. She was surrounded by friends and family—her husband, a Methodist clergyman; her parents, and her sister who came up from Virginia where she was in seminary. "I had spent a lot of time avoiding theological school," Victoria admitted, "mostly from the perspective that *anything* my sister did, I was *not* going to do. But by then, I had completed two years of seminary. And I was very pleased that Nancy had agreed to take part. I felt that it had to happen in order for the rest of us to be ordained."

Nancy Hatch Wittig

The first years after the Philadelphia ordination were difficult for both Hatch sisters, as they were for all the women ordained that day. The publicity, rejection by former friends, and the church's refusal to recognize the ordinations exacted a heavy spiritual and psychological toll. Nancy returned to Newark where she was prohibited from functioning as a priest until early 1977 when her ordination was regularized. Vicky applied for ordination to the diaconate in the Diocese of Virginia and was turned down for academic reasons. After passing the general ordination examinations, she reapplied and was ordained deacon in 1975, but she could not find a job in Virginia. Parishes wanted curates who would soon become priests and there was no assurance that ordination of women would pass General Convention. Finally, a seminary friend suggested her name to a California church. She was hired as a crisis center counselor and parish worker at St. Cross Church in the Diocese of Los Angeles, where she was subsequently ordained, becoming the first woman priest in that diocese.

Today, Nancy Hatch Wittig is rector of the Church of St. John the Divine in Hasbrouck Heights, New Jersey. "I never thought I would have the opportunity to be rector of a parish," she admitted. "I suspected that all of my professional life, because of Philadelphia, I would be a 'wandering Aramaean' as it were, but that was not true. I had always known that I would enjoy the parish ministry, and indeed, even on bad days, I love what I do."

The parish is a struggling, working-class church with about two hundred communicants. Many members are former Roman Catholics and a large percentage are women. "Because it is not fashionable for blue-collar Roman Catholics to switch over to the Episcopal Church, the men of the families remain nominal Catholics but allow their wives and children to come to St. John's. The economics of that is that the women pledge out of their own salaries, rather than the family's income, creating a situation of marginal economic growth," Wittig explained. The church is not able to provide a full-time salary for her and has no funds for secretarial assistance.

Making ends meet on an eighty-per-cent salary is hard for Wittig as a divorced woman with two children—twelve-year-old Alexandria and nine-year-old Wesley. Though the children's father is nearby and sees them regularly, they live with their mother. "It's very difficult to be a working mother in this society, and even more difficult if one is also a priest. My time does not coincide with the children's time off; they are off weekends while I have to work. What I try to do is to be who I am with them, giving them time and energy and love and attention in the same way I attend to my responsibilities as the local parish priest. I have learned how to juggle time and energy, but there are moments when I feel there is simply not enough time or energy to go around."

Why does she remain in such a job? "I care deeply for these people. In the last ten years, they have had four different rectors. It is a parish that did not take itself seriously and so it couldn't afford to take its clergy seriously. But that is changing. This year I am asking the congregational leaders to look seriously at their own faith journeys and begin to share those stories with each other openly. It's a kind of old fashioned evangelism; but I think that is what we need right now."

Across the United States in California, Victoria Hatch is working in a situation very similar to that of her sister. For the last ten years, she has been vicar of St. Agnes Church in Banning, California, a small town on the edge of the southern California desert, not far from Palm Springs. Though the church had been in Banning for many years, the congregation was small and, when Hatch arrived, most of the parishioners were senior citizens. During her years there, she has brought a number of young professionals—mainly educators—into the church and begun a Sunday school and a youth program for their children. Several Mexican-American families are now active. But the size of the congregation has increased only slightly. Average attendance on Sunday morning is thirty-five people. The congregation is not yet self-supporting.

"I am the only paid staff person and thereby must ultimately cover the waterfront in terms of responsibilities, from preaching to planning, from celebrating to teaching, from youth group director to pastoral counselor, and up and down the spectrum by which we define ministry. I feel a great deal of the time like the Mad Hatter from *Alice in Wonderland* crying 'I'm late, I'm late, for a very important date,'" Hatch said. "The most challenging work I'm doing right now is with the youth program—trying to plan with the young people, enjoying their spontaneity while setting an example of responsibility and accountability, and letting them know that the success or failure of the program is as much up to them as to me."

Her greatest frustration is the lack of numerical growth in the congregation. "The diocesan missions office measures success and failure solely on the basis of numbers—more confirmations, increased attendance at services, larger pledges. I think I have been able to accomplish a great deal here in terms of community building, of helping people see (and act out) that the church is not an *exclusive* but an *inclusive* organization, and that God's grace is there for everyone. But every step forward within the congregation is always accompanied by two steps backward in a put down by the missions office. There have been times when I thought that beating my head against a brick wall would accomplish more than trying to build up the kingdom of God," she said.

Last spring, the diocese cut Hatch's position from full time to half time without any consultation with her. Though she objected, her protests fell on deaf ears. "I was not given any reason for the change," she said. "I will be responsible and accountable for my behavior and my actions in dealing with parishioners and the hierarchy. But I don't believe that I did anything that warranted the treatment or the action that was taken."

Recognizing that the untimely death of Bishop Rusack had led to a great deal of uncertainty in the diocesan office, Hatch decided to make the best of a difficult situation, at least until a new diocesan bishop was elected. She continued as half-time vicar at St. Agnes. To support herself, she took a job teaching English and history at a nearby junior high school. "I am not going to let myself be forced out," she said. "I feel very strongly about small parishes, small rural or urban struggling places like St. Agnes, required to meet imposed criteria that are unrealistic and ultimately destructive. So I look upon this period as a breathing space for me. Though I want to be as involved as I can be in the diocese, I have discovered that when you rattle cages, you get bit!"

Within the diocese, she has had many supporters. In 1982 and 1985, the diocesan convention elected her as one of the four clergy deputies to General Convention. As one nearby vicar said, "I'm proud to be an associate of Vicky's and any woman who ministers as lovingly and faithfully to her little flock as she does. She does as I do—lives with a small, difficult, isolated group of the followers of Christ, day in, day out, come what may. She doesn't aspire (though she hopes!) and just slogs out the ministry. As a daily compatriot in the small church hassle, her consistent witness of caring and presence counts for a lot."

Thus, ten years after their ordinations, both sisters find themselves in tough situations, working in communities where the upward mobility of the American dream has simply been stalled. Hatch likens Banning to a ghetto community disguised as suburban

Americana. Wittig finds in Hasbrouck Heights the older folks have to stay because that's where their jobs are; their children, when they marry, have to move because they can't afford to live in the area. "It produces a world view that is very limited," she said. "People want to protect themselves from whatever horribleness is happening in other places. They want to keep the family safe, they want to keep themselves safe, and they want to do better than their parents. And they can't! So that produces a tremendous hunger for something beyond that."

Both sisters agree that meeting "tremendous hunger" is what the church is all about, and both have been willing to continue to invest their lives in the work before them. One of the factors that keeps them in their positions is that mobility for women priests is limited. Hatch has been the runner-up in three searches for rector. Wittig knows she needs to find a position with a full-time salary.

"A lot of women priests are being relegated to the small, marginal parishes, places where nobody else wants to be," said Wittig. "I think we can turn that fact into a positive, not only for ourselves but for Christ's ministry. That means we have to be taken seriously by the hierarchy. We must be taken seriously by each other and by ourselves. That means the small, struggling parishes that we serve must also be taken seriously by the church. We must see that no congregation is so small that the God of creation, the God of Jesus the Christ, cannot be found healing, redeeming and working out the divine purpose."

Beyond the low salary and lack of mobility and the church's insensitivity to the needs of small parishes, however, stands a deeper reality for both women. "I have an overwhelming sense that I am doing what I was put on this planet to do," explained Victoria Hatch. "It feels so right. Though I am not perfect, there are moments when I know that God uses me to touch other people's lives." Nancy Wittig agrees: "One of the marvelous realities of growing up as a daughter of the Episcopal Church is that so much is a part of you and you don't even know it. I think of the marvelous reality that the psalmists proclaim when they describe the relation between God and the earth. I know that this God of Creation, an ennobling and empowering God, calls us men and women to stand tall and to show forth in our lives the divine image, the compassion, love, and fullness that is so readily available and possible for each one of us. That knowledge sustains and empowers me."

Martha Johnston Horne

Send out your light and your truth, that they may lead me, and bring me to your holy hill and to your dwelling;

Psalm 43, The Ordination of a Priest

"Being a priest gives me the opportunity to be involved with people as they seek to find meaning in life; it keeps me actively engaged in the ultimate questions of human existence. Often I have no real answer to the questions: I don't know why innocent and good people suffer; I don't know why the evil prosper; I don't know why earthquakes and fires and famines and floods destroy vast populations. What I do know—and what I constantly must learn anew—is that there is ultimate meaning and truth in the answers I find in the Christian gospel. And I know that it is my task and my privilege to help others to apprehend the truth that is contained in that message."

As the assistant to the dean of Virginia Theological Seminary, Martha Johnston Horne conveys the gospel to those who are soon to be ordained. Like most educators, she balances a complex of many roles—teacher, student, administrator, counselor—in her relationships with students and faculty. Her administrative assignments include oversight of the admissions process, the planning and support of programs for seminary spouses, and the coordination of special events, particularly the annual Conference on Ministry which brings about one hundred prospective students and spouses to the campus for a weekend meeting.

In addition, she teaches one or two courses each semester. This semester she is assisting with the introductory New Testament course taken by all first-year students. Last year she taught elementary New Testament Greek and joined with three others to teach human sexuality. Teaching is her great love; next fall she hopes to begin courses for a doctoral degree to pursue a teaching career within the church. "I have taught Greek for most of the twenty-nine years that I have been at the seminary," said Dean

Martha Johnston Horne

Richard Reid, "and I can say without qualification that Martha is the best Greek student I ever had. She is also a very gifted teacher, who has been most affirmed in her classes."

Along with teaching, Horne serves as the faculty advisor to nine middler students and is faculty mentor for their field education colloquy. "Each week we take turns presenting 'event accounts' from our various parishes; the group then helps the presentor to identify and consider the practical, theological, and personal issues of ministry involved in the event."

How would Horne characterize theological education today? "Students come here with many different perspectives. And the great majority of them leave with broader visions and deeper understandings of ministry and of themselves in ministry—of the nature of God and of the nature of creation. That, to me, is exciting—but it is very slow work."

The fall semester has been a difficult semester for Horne. She has seen a retrenchment around the general issue of women in ministry that produced an unexpected polarization on campus. Other seminaries have reported similar unrest, triggered possibly by the trial use of a new liturgy written in inclusive language and presenting feminine as well as masculine images of God.

"All the seminaries were asked to use this liturgy on a trial basis for three weeks," Horne explained, "and then to evaluate its strengths and weaknesses, sending comments and suggestions back to the Standing Liturgical Commission. However, many students did not understand the process, and because (through a coincidence in scheduling) I happened to be the first celebrant to use the inclusive language liturgy, some students assumed I was pushing it." Horne went on to explain that although she favored greater attention to inclusive language, she felt that the trial use liturgy had some serious flaws. The use of that liturgy by the community touched deeply held emotional assumptions about the nature of God and raised some unsettling questions for some students and faculty. "We need to be able to talk about these questions in a nonthreatening, nondivisive way," said Horne, "and we haven't been able to do so yet."

Other faculty members are also concerned. The Virginia faculty members have been very supportive of ordination of women to the priesthood. They, with the Board of Trustees have recently issued a statement, reiterating the seminary's position that its primary mission is "to prepare men and women for the ordained ministry, particularly for service in the parish ministry and leadership in the church." Currently one-third of the master of divinity candidates at Virginia are women. Though Horne is the only ordained woman on the faculty, Marianne H. Micks is professor of biblical and historical theology and B. Barbara Hall is professor of New Testament.

Being a part of such a supportive community is important to Horne. Living on campus is one great advantage of her seminary position. She loves being able to walk to work; her teenage sons, Christopher and Peter, attend St. Stephen's School, a short walk from the seminary grounds. "When this position came up, I consulted them first because if they had not wanted to move, I don't think I would have pursued it. But they were very enthusiastic about coming; they had fond memories of the seminary when I was a student here," she explained. Her husband, McDonald K. Horne III, is a physician, a research hematologist employed at the National Institutes of Health in Bethesda. Though his commute is about forty minutes each way, the fact that he has regular hours and is on call only every fourth weekend allows ample time for family activities.

It was not always so. After graduating from seminary, Horne took a part-time position in a parish in order to leave herself more time with her family. "Unfortunately, I failed to recognize how difficult it is to do part-time ministry," she admitted. "No matter how carefully one tries to structure one's time, inevitably the scheduled 'time off' is the time when crises occur, or when something particularly interesting is happening in the parish. In addition, my sons were growing up quickly, and I did not want to miss being a part of their growth and development."

Though her family responsibilities led her away from parish ministry, she found the work itself stimulating and enriching. For four years, she worked as assistant to Randall Prior at St. Andrew's Church in Burke, Virginia. "During that time we became aware of how much the congregation seemed to enjoy and appreciate the ways in which we worked together as a man and a woman. I began to hear from people that it just didn't 'feel right' when either of us was away on a Sunday morning. There seemed to be a genuine sense of well-being and security generated when we taught a class together, or celebrated the Eucharist."

Prior echoed this assessment, saying, "I think the main learning for me was the importance of a male-female staff team for the parish. Martha was able to do things for the women and for the men of the parish that I was unable to do, and vice versa. I'm convinced that the dynamic of having both male and female representation on a clergy staff signifies something very important about the wholeness of humanity." When Horne left, he hired another woman priest.

Horne moved from that parish to a full-time position as associate rector at Christ Church, Alexandria. One of her responsibilities there was working with a weekly Bible study group of young women. "Over the course of our time together many of these women became pregnant. Several gave birth to healthy babies which they brought along to our meetings. Others suffered miscarriages, and found themselves helped to bear their loss by the compassion and caring of friends who visited them, cooked for them, prayed for them and cried with them. It was a great privilege and joy for me to share with them the particular tribulations and joys of motherhood. And I think it was important for them to have me with them, not only as another woman, wife and mother, but also as a priest. They were able to hear and respond to the gospel in new ways when we read scripture together and reflected on its implications for us as Christian women. My presence at the altar each Sunday seemed to give them more of a sense of being represented there themselves."

Since accepting the seminary position, she has continued to be affiliated with Christ Church as priest associate, taking services the last Sunday of each month, teaching two adult education courses each year and doing some pastoral work. "In a parish of our size (some 2,000 communicants) and in an area where there are a great many educated and articulate women, a woman on the staff is imperative," said the rector, Mark S. Anschutz. "I've been gradually won over to this position, primarily because of the grace, wisdom, and effectiveness of Martha Horne."

Though she was the first woman priest to serve at either St. Andrew's or Christ Church, in both cases she was warmly welcomed. "I know that it has not been easy for many people to accept the presence of women in the pulpit or at the altar," she admitted, "but I have been spared some of the terribly painful forms of rejection that many of my sister priests have experienced."

One of the problems that concerns Horne as she works with prospective clergy is the matter of competition: competition between men and women for positions of authority and competition among women. Recently, within her own support group of clergywomen, two of the members were candidates for rector of a nearby parish and one was called. "Although there were no lingering ill effects, and the candidates are still friends and supporters of each other, I saw the potential for mistrust and broken relationships. I think this presents a challenge and an opportunity for us to foresee and deal constructively with a significant issue. Perhaps, as women, we can model a new way of dealing with competition."

These and other issues concerning women in ministry will continue to be of particular concern to Martha Horne. She is committed to the best theological education possible for women and men. She is convinced that there are still complex questions surrounding the theological dimensions of a priesthood that includes women as well as men and the ways in which such a priesthood will shape and perhaps alter our understanding of the nature of God. These are profound and potentially disturbing questions that must be discussed and examined in an atmosphere of mutual trust and respect. But above all, she finds her work at the seminary "very gratifying. I feel blessed to have the opportunity to serve God in this way, and I pray that my identity as a person and priest will enable others to find the direction of their own ministries."

Rachel Hosmer at General Theological Seminary with the late Bishop William Dimmick

Rachel Hosmer

For all members of your Church in their vocation and ministry, that they may serve you in a true and godly life, we pray to you, O Lord.

The Litany for Ordinations

"My call to ministry came sometime in the twenties, before I entered religious life in 1928. It had to do with the desire to know, understand and minister to the poor. My call to ordination could be dated somewhere in the seventies when the possibility first came to my consciousness and when several people asked me to consider it."

Thus, with characteristic conciseness, Rachel Hosmer summarized God's call to her, and in so doing, she encapsulated a lifetime's vocation in God's service—first as professed sister and later as deacon and priest. Hosmer entered the Order of St. Anne in 1928, made her profession of life vows in 1935 and in 1945 became a founding member and first sister in charge of the Order of St. Helena. In 1975 she was ordained deacon and two years later priest in the Diocese of New York. At seventy-nine, she works as an adjunct professor and spiritual director at the General Theological Seminary in New York, while living at the Convent of St. Helena and participating in the community life there.

At the seminary, Hosmer offers two weekly prayer groups: a silent centering group and a monastic breakfast. The silent group meets in the evening after chapel. "We begin with the salutation and a little yoga—spiritual exercise," Sister Rachel explained. "We use the image of 'the cloud of unknowing'—letting words and images drop and letting just one word carry our love through the cloud of unknowing. We sit together in the dim room in silence. Before we begin, I ask if we have any special intercessions and at the end, I ask that we pick up those intercessions and just hold them before God. After a brief intercessory prayer, we say the 'Our Father' together. Then we turn up the lights and have a simple supper—cheese and crackers and fruit and something to drink. Chatting together over food helps to form a community."

The monastic breakfast meets Tuesday mornings from 6:30 to 7:30. People come to be together in silence. Some people read, some pray. At the end of the period, they all share a line or two of whatever they have on their minds. With the phrase, "Christ is in the midst of us, alleluia," the group shares a simple breakfast and then goes on to Morning Prayer. Participation in both groups is open to all—seminarians, spouses, faculty—with no required attendance commitment. "I say, come if you want to pray together in silence. My students say, 'Rachel thinks we come to pray but what we really do is come to eat,' she laughed.

Hosmer also works privately with a number of people as their spiritual director. "We begin with a mutual exploration of what the person wants to work on so that I can make my mind up if I think I can be helpful, or if I should refer them to someone else. If they want to go on, then we make a definite agreement about regular meetings—usually every three weeks. The chief thing I do is to keep the whole thing centered on God. How do you hear God in your situation? What do you pray about? What do you sense that God is replying to you? These are the questions I raise. We do talk about where to use prayer and silence in the day if they have questions about that. There's not any pattern on that level. It's personal."

"I consider Sister Rachel to be a holy person—tough, but open to the spirit in a remarkable way," said James C. Fenhagen, dean of General Seminary. "I have been with her in an early morning meditation group for some time and have been touched by her wisdom, faithfulness, and her continual support of my ministry."

The dean's words are echoed by faculty members, seminarians, priests and lay people with whom Sister Rachel works. "Rachel has always challenged me to expand my horizons," said Elisabeth Koenig, who teaches ascetical theology. "The way she integrates her intellectual grasp of theology, scripture, and tradition with her experience of spirituality and her intense involvement with the peace movement is quite remarkable."

Rachel admits that her most challenging work is being a spiritual director and preaching in the seminary chapel. "My most frustrating tasks are, and always have been, household work, for which I have no aptitude nor taste but which I am glad to do as my share of the community life. Also vexing is my work with the diocesan task force on peace. I think peace work is very painful and difficult and frustrating in the world as it is today."

Within that world, she has had an extraordinarily broad range of experience. After graduating from Boston University with a major in ancient languages, she taught at Margaret Hall, a secondary boarding school for girls operated by the Order of St. Anne in Kentucky (later operated by the Order of St. Helena). Sister Rachel had entered the Order of St. Anne before she finished her university degree and made her life profession while at Margaret Hall. In 1935 she was made principal and continued in that position for the next quarter century. While setting high academic standards, she also tried to develop self-confidence and a social conscience in her young charges.

An increasing awareness of the church's worldwide mission led her to Africa in 1962, where she worked as principal of St. Philip and St. Agnes School at the Holy Cross Mission in Bolahun, Liberia. That experience was a jolting culture shock for her. "My first impression was that it was so hot and so damp, how was I going to be able to live and breathe. We flew into Bolahun from Monrovia in a little-bitty plane—five people. Crowds of people came out to meet us and they took us to the church and we got blessed in. It was so different from my expectations; it was terrifying. For the first week, I was very frightened."

Gradually she discarded all her previously formed images of what American sisters might do for the Liberian people and began to see and appreciate the richness and the beauty of the African culture. "I learned that I was there to discover what God had already done in that place. I came to love the work deeply. When my order recalled me to the United States, I did not want to leave. I hated leaving. I cried," she said, remembering how she asked the driver not to take her by the school because she couldn't bear to see the children's faces as she left.

Except for one furlough home, she had been in Africa from 1962 until 1971, teaching in various schools and finally helping implement the process of transferring the administration of the Bolahun mission to the Liberians.

On her return to the United States, she spent one semester as campus minister at Georgia Southern University in Statesboro, Georgia, then moved back to the Convent of St. Helena in New York. Living there she worked part time as program director at Calvary Church while teaching Bible at the Baptist Educational Center.

The possibility of seeking priesthood came into her mind most forcibly one day in the early 1970s when she served on a panel at Union Seminary. "Someone in the audience addressed me personally, saying, 'How would your community feel if you were to be ordained deacon? It would be helpful to us if some of the older religious women who are respected in the church were to be ordained.' And I suddenly thought, that is a good idea." She and two other sisters of St. Helena—Mary Michael Simpson and

Columba Gilliss—brought the issue before the next chapter meeting, asking permission to seek the diaconate with the understanding that if the church provided for ordination to priesthood, they would go on. The order granted the permission and all three have been subsequently ordained priest. Hosmer entered General Seminary and completed her S.T.M. In June, 1975, she was ordained deacon and two years later, in April, 1977, she was ordained priest.

Intellectual inquiry has always been important to Sister Rachel. Combining a wide knowledge of ancient cultures and Biblical history with contemporary issues, she has made an extensive study of Christian attitudes and responses to poverty. Presently she is working on a comparison of the positions of pentecostal fundamentalism with those of the Episcopal Church on such issues as peace, justice and ecology.

What personal rewards has Sister Rachel found in priesthood? "It gives me joy to celebrate, to lead worship, to visit the sick and dying, to hear confessions, and to preach. I find it rewarding also to be part of the counsels of the church and diocesan convention. I've enjoyed taking part as an equal in mutual ministry in conversation with male priests who take me seriously, as well as with women. It's deeply satisfying trying to minister to special needs—to find or devise liturgical expressions for the ministry of healing.

"Let me add something about being a priest within a religious order: I am grateful that in spite of the fact that a few of our members cannot accept the priestly ministry of those of us who are ordained, they have never tried to block us. From the beginning, when the possibility of my ordination was first discussed, they said their reluctance was their problem, they did not want us to curtail our activities in the convent. It is painful, this division, but it could be a lot worse. It is not ugly, but rather a mutual respect of differences."

Does she think that religious orders will disappear now that women can be ordained priest? "No," she said, "though it seems to be true that we are losing applicants since the priesthood has been open to women. Monastic life is a distinct vocation and if we live it faithfully, it will not fail the church. It's been in the church from the earliest days. God must have put it there. God raised it up. And God will keep on raising it up if God wants it. Monasticism is a gift—a charism within the church. I wouldn't want to see it disappear, and I don't think it will.''

Margaret Smith Hutchins

That I may go to the altar of God,
to the God of my joy and gladness;
and on the harp I will give thanks to you, O God my God."

Psalm 43, The Ordination of a Priest

"Even in so-called 'liberal' dioceses such as Connecticut, there are still too many people who have not accepted as valid the ministry of ordained women," said Margaret Hutchins. "Personally, I feel that the 'conscience clause' is unconscionable, probably illegal and certainly morally wrong. It is painful for me to feel that my ministry, which feels so right to me, afflicts the conscience of any other Christian. I have never considered myself a raging feminist but I am so tired of always having to explain myself to the uncomprehending and the unconcerned. I am tired of being polite about generic language, tired of being patronized, put down or ignored, and tired of being considered 'pushy' if I have a good idea or 'passive' if I don't."

Margaret Smith Hutchins is a forthright and determined priest. In May, 1987, some Connecticut Episcopalians, dismayed that the election committee's nominations for suffragan bishop did not include any women, took it upon themselves to nominate Hutchins for that position. A woman in her mid-fifties, she had been active in the diocese for many years and had served as priest in four congregations since her ordination in 1981. The fact that she had not followed the traditional model of moving from small mission to larger parish to eventual candidacy for bishop was hailed as an advantage by those who nominated her. As the Reverend Byron David Stuhlman stated, "Unlike most candidates for the episcopate, Margaret spent most of her adult life as a committed lay Christian in a wide variety of parishes across the country. This gives her an 'insider's view' on the place of laity in the church which is quite different from that of the majority of the church's clergy, who have spent most of their adult lives in the ordained ministry."

At the convention, two women—Margaret Hutchins and Patricia Davidson—were among the twelve nominees. Neither was elected but both received a credible number of votes. Admitting that she did not expect to be elected, Margaret Hutchins stressed that nevertheless she did think it was important that the diocese be given the opportunity to consider a woman candidate. How did she feel during the process? "It was a terrible strain. We appeared before the delegates in four different parts of the state. I hate being the center of attention, having people throwing questions at you. Folks who were there said I handled it very well." Did she even allow herself to consider the possibility of being elected? "Oh, yes. There is a part of me that said, 'Hey, wouldn't that be nice—to be the first woman bishop.' And then I'd think, 'Oh, no, the hounding by the press, the hounding by those who don't believe women should even be ordained! And the work load itself—it's a heavy, heavy work load. What would the job do to my home life?' And yet, I really did feel called to let my name stand. If God was actually calling me to do this job, God would provide the strength to do it.''

The call to ordained ministry takes many forms. For Margaret Hutchins it came as a persistent growing sense of personal vocation in the midst of a family who participated actively in church activities. ''I am a 'cradle' Episcopalian, the oldest of three living children, daughter of a clergyman. Religion was an integral part of our family life—not so much talked about as just there—and most of our outside activities centered in parish life. I did all the things which girls of my generation could do—Sunday school, choir, Young People's Fellowship, etc. I really enjoyed these activities and clearly they were the basis of my ongoing interest in things 'churchy.' I just absorbed this ecclesiastical learning into my system so that it became such a part of me that often I am not even aware of its presence.''

Margaret was raised at a time, however, when few women even considered the possibility of ordination. Graduating from college in the midst of the ''togetherness generation'' of the early 1950s, she married Walter the day after graduation and ''began our lives as 'corporate gypsies'—fourteen addresses in twenty-one years—sixteen parishes in eleven dioceses. Always, one of the first things to be done after finding a new house was to find a new parish and establish a life within it. Sometimes this was easy and comfortable, sometimes difficult and rather painful, but it was very important because in many ways it was the church which provided me with a sense of stability and continuity, giving me the strength to provide the stability which our frequently-uprooted family life needed to survive intact.''

While Walter worked as an engineer for General Electric, Margaret spent those early years as a housewife and mother. Four children—Katharine, Elizabeth, Laurie, and James—were born during the next twelve years.

''As the family needed less and less of my time, I found myself becoming even more involved in church activities. However, I had no conscious sense of a call to ordination, only a slowly deepening sense of commitment to the church and then, gradually, a growing awareness of the reality of God's presence in my life...something which I hadn't thought much about until the family experienced a very difficult time. Problems related to employment, raising teenagers, marriage, and the death of two parents all combined to create what seemed to be an interminable period of discord and unhappiness. When the worst of all that abated and I could breathe again, I began to realize that my commitment to the church and my awareness of God's immediate presence were beginning to come together in a way which was focusing on priesthood."

Deciding at least to explore the idea, Margaret Hutchins entered the Episcopal Divinity School in Cambridge, Massachusetts, in 1977. As a full-time student, she lived on campus during the week and commuted home to West Hartford, Connecticut, each weekend. "It was rough, but it will remain one of the highlights of my life," she testified. Going through the process of becoming a candidate for ordination from the Diocese of Connecticut was also difficult, "but I survived with the support of family, friends and faith."

Since her ordination in 1981, Margaret has worked as vicar of a small rural congregation (Christ Church, Harwinton) and then as interim in three locations (a campus chaplain and vicar at St. Mark's, Storrs; St. Peter's Church, South Windsor; and St. Paul's Church, New Haven). She is presently at St. Paul's Church in Wallingford. The role of interim minister is a difficult one; the priest must carry out the regular administrative, liturgical and pastoral responsibilities of rector in a parish that is often "grieving or seething or burned out." As Margaret explained, "I must go in as a stranger, quickly build some trust, plow some ground, plant some seeds and then leave quietly. I often remark that being an interim is like being John the Baptist—although I still have my head! The most frustrating thing I face is that the work is so often viewed as not quite authentic ministry, not quite 'real.' I can't tell you how often I have been asked—by clergy as well as laity—'When are you going to get a real job?'" How does she deal with that attitude? "I simply try to do the best job I can in whatever place I find myself."

Doing that job is not always easy. Her present parish is a thirty-minute drive from home—a long drive at night after a vestry meeting. It is hard to find time to spend with her husband. "Any two-career family has scheduling problems, but with the clergy, it's worse. There go your weekends! And since any more it seems that the only time to do church business is at night, there go your evenings. I find myself just real tired at Christmas and Easter, those times where previously I would have been planning all kinds of family festivities. The load comes heavier on the clergywoman because rarely does she have the kind of a spouse who will take over and do all those other things she always did for the holidays. Every so often Walter will say to me with a plaintive note in his voice, 'You know what I miss more than anything else is those Sunday morning breakfasts you used to cook.'"

The interim placements have meant, however, that the family could stay in the West Hartford house. "After moving so often for so many years, Walter and I have both told everyone the only way we'll leave that house is when we're carried out," she asserts. Though she has little time for community activities, Hutchins does continue to sing in the Hartford Chorale, which does three major concerts each year. "Music is very important to me. I've sung in choirs since I was in the second grade. Working on serious music with that group is a wonderful release for me."

Margaret's interim work has also introduced congregations to the possibility of calling women rectors. Parishioners find her energy and personal vitality refreshing; she makes the faith come alive in a very special way. As Junior Warden George A. Potterton explained, the members of St. Peter's Church were won over by Margaret's spiritual commitment and her understanding and caring. "She was a good teacher—intellectually stimulating—and she conducted services with enthusiasm. We were impressed by her devotion to her calling, which inspired us to have faith in the continuation toward a self-supporting parish. The fact that we called a lady—the Reverend Sara Chandler—as our new rector was undoubtedly due to Margaret's ministry among us."

Supporting other clergywomen is important to Hutchins. As a member of the Steering Committee for Women Clergy of the diocese, she serves as both political agitator and friendly counsel for Connecticut clergywomen—of whom there are presently about fifty. "Though there is a tendency to think of women clergy as a unit, sharing the same concerns and hopes and dreams, that isn't true. We, like the men, are divided. But some of us are willing to stand up and work together for changes. In many ways this diocese is good old fashioned New England Yankee—they just hang in there, don't want to change."

What are Hutchins' plans for the future? "Right now I am working with the canon to the ordinary on the whole issue of interim ministry. If we are going to continue to use the kind of calling process we have been using, we must be more intentional about the interims. I plan to write some diocesan guidelines for such ministries—and share them with other dioceses. Personally, I want to continue doing interim ministry. I like it. I have the gifts for it. People ask me if I'd like to be the rector of a church. If the right kind of situation came along, I probably would, but I find myself being very picky about what that situation might be. For the present, my challenge is to help the church enlarge and develop its concept of interim ministry."

Rosanna Case Kazanjian

Will you undertake to be a faithful pastor to all whom you are called to serve, laboring together with them and with your fellow ministers to build up the family of God?

The Examination

"To be priest is to be a healer, a shaman. You will be in the presence of much brokenness, individual and community. You will not survive this hard and wonderful work unless you make room in your life for joy, play, renewal, and alternation. You will need to hold gently the paradox of this work; you are very important to the work. You are called and sent and you are one—only one—of God's creatures and there are many others called and sent. There are many others with hands and hearts to help. Remember to dance, holding hands, eye to eye, in the mutuality to which we are all called. Remember to ask for help. Remember, limits recognized are great strengths. Most of all remember, like Miriam, to dance with timbral and harp as a response to God. In all you are called to do with your life and ministry, keep before you God's promise through Isaiah and Jesus, 'I am here, follow me.'"

Thus, Rosanna Kazanjian concluded her advice to her son, Victor, as she preached the sermon at his ordination to the priesthood in May, 1987. In a sense, the ceremony was the culmination of a dual journey. She had been ordained just two years earlier; her last year at the Episcopal Divinity School in Cambridge was her son's second year there. For both, life at seminary was shadowed by a profound family crisis—the death of Rosanna's husband, Victor, from cancer in 1985. The family's experience of dealing with his suffering and death gave them a sense of their own deep spiritual resources. Young Victor's ordination was a bittersweet family occasion, full of much joy and many memories.

The words of the sermon reflected an understanding of priesthood shaped in part by the particular circumstances of Rosanna's

Rosanna Case Kazanjian

ministry, for she has been, for the past two years, the only Episcopal woman functioning as a parish priest in the Diocese of Dallas. Traditionally a "high church" diocese, Dallas included among its priests many men who were adamantly opposed to the ordination of women. Not until after 1983 when the diocese was divided (making the dioceses of Dallas and Fort Worth) and a new bishop, Donis D. Patterson, took office, were women allowed to function as priests in the diocese. Though Kazanjian knew this history when she agreed to come to Texas, she was not personally prepared for the depth of the animosity and fear she found in many of the priests there.

"For reasons I am not quite sure of, I got called to Richardson, Texas, and felt that was where I was supposed to come. And it has been an exciting, fruitful, demanding, sometimes deeply saddening experience because this diocese is very troubled. Half of its clergy are really terribly opposed to women's ordination. They are pretty vocal and sometimes ugly about it." Facing such opposition forced her to come to terms with her own sense of priesthood, to define her own concept of ministry. Her words to Victor spelled out that definition: Ministry is healing. It is mutual—recognizes and calls forth the gifts of others. And it is done with joy—listening to and informed by the rhythm of the world.

"When I'm invited to other churches in the dioceses to talk about women's ordination, I say to them, that is no longer the issue. We've settled that in the church; women priests are a reality. Now what we need to do together is to experience ourselves as men and women in ministry, to ask ourselves how we can serve God and Jesus Christ in ways that are full and creative and imaginative—ways that move us into a deeper relationship with each other and with God. This business of women in ministry is not a matter of superwomen, or doing it right, or being extraordinary, but of entering into the communion of Christian work together, bringing whatever freshness we can, as women, to that work," she explained.

Her own maturity and good sense in dealing with this issue has enabled her to be an effective advocate of women in priesthood. "Rosanna is, to me, an example of the medium being the message. She has accepted and taken into herself the fear, anger, hatred, and vituperation of those who seem unalterably opposed to women in the priesthood, and she has allowed the indwelling Spirit of God to transform those hurtful, negative, abusive insults. What remains in her and what she gives back are compassion and understanding and love for those who would be her enemies," said parishioner Elizabeth Hudson.

Rosanna serves as the associate rector of the Church of the Epiphany in Richardson. Epiphany is a large, rapidly growing congregation in one of the more affluent suburbs of Dallas. It's a high-church congregation, but one with a wide range of liturgical usages, from folk mass to chanted high mass. Average church attendance is about six hundred each Sunday; the Sunday school has about three hundred pupils and teachers. Adult Christian education classes are offered also on Wednesday nights. There are junior and senior high youth groups and an active acolyte program. Women's organizations include the Daughters of the King, the Episcopal Church Women and a variety of guilds. A men's club meets for dinner twice a month. "It's an informal, family-centered congregation. People are not fancy in their dressing or in their life style but the church is really at the center of their lives in a way I've never seen before," Kazanjian said.

The clergy staff—Kazanjian; Steve White, the rector; and Richard Spear, the assistant for youth ministry—have sought to establish a model for working together that emphasizes their mutual ministry. The tasks of preaching and being chief celebrant at the Sunday Eucharist are shared equally. Steve has the main responsibility for administrative tasks; Richard coordinates youth programs; Rosanna focuses on counseling, teaching, spiritual direction, and incorporation of new members. She also teaches adult courses and works with leaders of parish organizations.

Maintaining such professional partnerships requires constant scrutiny. "The pit we fall into most easily is that we duplicate the cultural norms about women being the nurturers and men being the administrators," said Kazanjian. "I keep finding myself being the supporter, the person who backs up the rector and fills in where he can't be. I need to be constantly intentional about my own creative role in shaping this community. And Steve wants more time for the nurturing and encouraging roles. We're both committed to team ministry but it is terribly frustrating to try to change the long-standing habits and customs that have governed working relationships between men and women."

The importance of the model of working together is not lost to parishioners. One woman described the profound healing that began as she took part in the Sunday Eucharists administered by the two priests. Her childhood had been full of unhappiness and insecurity caused by constant arguments and discord between her parents. But the presence in the sanctuary of a man and a woman working together in harmony demonstrated the wholeness of God's creation and brought peace to the warring elements within her.

Helping women discover and develop their spirituality is an area of special interest to Kazanjian. "Here in Texas, I've discovered how deep the prejudice is against the feminine in our culture, and yet how great the longing is for the men and women living out the wholeness of who they are." To explore these issues, she began a support group of women. It's an open group; people come and go, but with a fairly consistent core group of active parish leaders. Ages range from the twenties through the seventies. Meeting bi-weekly, these women share their spiritual journeys through such different forms as Bible study, dream analysis, or general group discussion. "I am constantly amazed at the openness of these strong, deeply spiritual women. Working with them has been a very special part of my ministry," Kazanjian said.

Kazanjian has found her position in the diocese quite isolated. Few of the other Episcopal priests have reached out to make any contacts with her. She has been invited to celebrate the Eucharist in only one other parish. In order to open lines of communication, Bishop Patterson called together a group of twelve priests evenly divided between those who favored and those who opposed ordination of women. "It is hard being the only woman in that group," Kazanjian said. "At one meeting, when we were each describing our call to the priesthood, I realized that after I finished speaking, half of the people in the room would not believe that what I said was valid. They listened to me, even cried with me as I spoke. But the next time I would see them at a diocesan function, I would feel again their sense of separation from me as a woman priest. I could feel their denial and fear."

Because of the isolation, Kazanjian has actively sought involvement in the larger community. She meets regularly with a group of women clergy of other denominations and welcomes the opportunity to discuss mutual problems in that supportive atmosphere. She has devoted some of her extracurricular time to the issue of world peace, working with a coalition of Dallas women planning a convocation for peace in August, 1988.

Kazanjian finds it difficult to be a single person in ministry. As a widow, she has found that the celibate life can be lonely. "I am trying to learn new ways of building healthy relationships and allowing myself to grow, but I don't find that easy. I think that being single cuts one off from some parts of the ministry. I have to be very sensitive and cautious in my ministry to men, particularly married men. When I was a married woman, that was never a problem. As a therapist, I had men as well as women clients but never felt uneasy about the sexual dimensions of the relationship. It is different for me now. This is one area that I would really like to have a chance to discuss with other single women priests."

She grew up as the daughter of a Methodist minister. While still in college, she married Victor Kazanjian, a young attorney. "I joined the Episcopal Church because of him. He had just been baptized and confirmed and it was clear that the church was a very powerful thing in his life. I wanted to be part of that with him." She and Victor eventually settled in Wellesley, Massachusetts. Over the next eight years they had three children: Victor, Helene and David. While spending the first few years of their marriage primarily as a housewife and mother, Rosanna became interested in the study of group dymanics and later worked as a consultant and trainer for the Diocese of Massachusetts.

After returning to college for a master's degree, she was hired as director of counseling at Dana Hall, a private girls' school in Wellesley. "As I worked with the young women and their parents and teachers at Dana Hall, I found that a good deal of the counseling I was doing was exploring with them, without necessarily using God language, the deeper meanings of life—who am I in relation to this universe? Who is in charge here? Where do I find my place in this world? My own faith deepened. I began to have a strong sense of a call which I tried to ignore. I did not want to give up a very successful profession and start a whole new one. I certainly did not want to go back to graduate school;

I am not an academician. So I fought against and tried to ignore the call."

Talking with a woman priest, Elsa Walberg, encouraged her to explore the possibility of ordination. She took a year's leave of absence from Dana Hall and entered the Episcopal Divinity School on a part-time basis. But just a few months into the fall term, they discovered her husband had cancer. "So that whole year of decision-making and sabbatical was turned toward our dealing with the trauma and ultimate tragedy of a very young man having cancer and not surviving it," she said.

Ultimately, with her husband's support, Kazanjian decided she did want to pursue priesthood. She returned to seminary and applied for candidacy in the Diocese of Massachusetts, all the while caring for Victor. He died two months before she graduated. "He was a confident, loving man who supported me absolutely in every step of the journey over the years as I gained confidence in myself as a woman—a long hard struggle. He believed in me long before I did and he always stood patiently waiting for me to get to a new place of self-acceptance. I had learned to move slowly, day by day, to say goodbye to a life of thirty-two years of marriage and to greet a new life opening up to me at the same time. I was both grateful and deeply saddened."

Because her family responsibilities had changed, she felt free to go wherever she was called. So when Stephen White, who had met her at the seminary while he was doing a graduate course, asked her to consider working with him at Epiphany, she agreed at least to be interviewed for the position.

"I immediately loved the energy here, and the openness and friendliness of the people. I knew it was the right place for me. I think I could not have found my own individual self either as a single person or as a priest in the same community I had lived in so long. And I will be grateful till the day I die to the people here because I think they have both helped me grow into my priesthood and helped shape it in ways I could never have imagined."

For the congregation, Rosanna Kazanjian has demonstrated that women can bring gifts to the priesthood. "Her greatest strength," said one parishioner, "is her profound relationship with the living God. Her spirituality seems to go to the very depths of her being, and it pours forth from her as naturally as water from a living spring. She is an *authentic* person, and by the quality of her living and being, she invites others also to be authentic persons. Before I knew Rosanna, it didn't matter to me that my parish had all male clergy. Now, I would feel a great *lack* if we did not have a woman priest or deacon."

Nan Arrington Peete

Will you endeavor so to minister the Word of God and the sacraments of the New Covenant, that the reconciling love of Christ may be known and received?

The Examination

"My grandmother, who died in 1953 at ninety years of age, told us we were special people and had an obligation to make life better for others. Special, not because we were rich materially, but because we had been well educated, had good families, love, and as children of God were blessed. Our well-being was tied to the well-being of others. Therefore, I took those words to mean I should be involved in community issues, and I was—from the civil rights and peace issues of the sixties to the school desegregation, police brutality, racism, and farm workers' issues in Los Angeles in the seventies. It also meant being involved in local community projects such as the Board of Directors of the Metropolitan Y.W.C.A., the Southern Christian Leadership Conference, the United Way Speakers Bureau and the Los Angeles School District Parent Advisory Board."

Nan Peete's eloquence is obvious as she describes her grandmother's legacy—an abiding spirit of social concern that eventually led Peete into the Episcopal priesthood. Nan Olive Arrington grew up in Chicago in the midst of a large extended family. Her mother was one of eleven children. Since grandmother Clanton lived with the Arringtons, that household became the social center for the aunts and uncles and cousins. Nan and her sister Edna felt secure in that home, educated and inspired by their frail, but inwardly strong, grandmother. Though grandmother was a Baptist, Nan's father, Maurice, was a long-time Episcopalian and her parents had been married in the Episcopal Church. After Nan and her sister were baptized, their insistence ultimately brought the Arringtons into active participation in the Episcopal Church.

Nan attended Chicago Teachers College in the fifties, but married Robert Peete and left school without finishing her degree. He was a writer for a Chicago advertising firm. They had two children—a son, Richard, and a daughter, Valerie. "I went back to work when Valerie was five weeks old," Peete relates. "I look now at my son who is twenty-seven. He has a good job in a high-tech computer company. He and his wife have an $80,000 house and two cars—when we were twenty-seven, we had two children, period!"

Robert's promotion in 1970 necessitated a move to Los Angeles. When the family arrived, they read about an Episcopal Church that had bolted its front doors, stating that they would not be reopened until the last American soldier returned from Vietnam.

The Peetes joined St. John's Church, finding that it "really practiced what it preached in terms of peace and justice. Eventually, Nan became senior warden and also served as director of the church's free neighborhood medical clinic. "It was in that church that I first felt called to priesthood. I was sitting in the midst of the service and I heard a voice saying 'You should be up there preaching.' And I really had an internal discussion saying, 'Not me,' like Isaiah. 'Woe is me, I am a sinner in your sight, what do I have to offer?' But then I thought, 'Why not?' So I started asking other people and I kept getting answers like, 'Well, we were wondering when you were going to decide' or 'What took you so long?' That sounds really arrogant but it was overwhelming to me that people felt that I had a calling to the ordained ministry."

To go to seminary at that time was difficult for Peete. She and Robert had separated. He had left the advertising company and was beginning to make his way as a screenwriter. "Being a writer is just very hard," she said, "and that was part of the problem in our relationship. His needs were the same as mine. Each of us just didn't have a lot to *give* each other."

Nan was living alone and working as a management consultant for an accounting firm, a job that required a great deal of traveling. With a son at Georgetown University and daughter at Spelman College in Atlanta, she needed the job. Fortunately, the Diocese of Los Angeles sponsored a seminary program at Bloy House where she could take classes on Friday evenings and all day Saturday. She enrolled in the fall of 1980 and attended classes there for two years, completing the first year's seminary requirements. She is very proud of the fact that she never missed a class and was only late once when she stayed late at work and got caught in a traffic jam on a Los Angeles freeway! She transferred to General in New York for her final two years.

Receiving her M. Div. degree in 1984, she returned to Los Angeles and became the first black woman to be ordained priest in that diocese, serving as curate at St. Mark's Church in Upland. "I replaced a woman who had been there for three years, so they looked forward to having another woman. It was very important for them to have a woman because they saw the fullness of God represented in the male and female clergy. So I was readily accepted. The fact that I was black and that was an all-white church, was not an issue. I had women who would come to me to discuss pastoral issues that they felt they could not go to their rector with. I think one of the things that the women bring to the ministry is the ability to listen and be empathetic and be available. With our vulnerability and our openness, women relate to people in a collegial rather than a competitive way."

After little more than a year as curate, Peete was called to be rector of All Saints Church in Indianapolis and moved there in 1985. Though it is located near downtown, as *the* anglo-catholic parish, All Saints draws members from throughout the city. "The congregation represents the broad spectrum of the body of Christ," said Peete. "We have relatively few children, several families, many singles—it's about thirty per cent black. Many people have been surprised that a high-church parish would call a woman priest because they think that anglo-catholics don't accept women priests. But I tell them that All Saints parish has a true sense of what catholicism means in terms of being universal and accepting of all people. They certainly have been most supportive of me and the work I've tried to do."

Calling itself a eucharistically centered, socially concerned congregation, All Saints is a member of the Indianapolis Episcopal Metropolitan Council (Metrocouncil). This thirteen-parish consortium sponsors a feeding ministry six days a week and a shelter for the homeless. All Saints houses the diocesan urban center. As rector, Peete administers this center, which rents office space to several community agencies at a lower rate than they could find elsewhere. About two hundred people are fed lunch each day in the parish house. The parish sponsors an after-school tutorial program for elementary school children.

In October, 1986, when a drastic drop in temperature highlighted the need for shelter for the homeless, Peete urged her congregation to open the church to those who had no place to sleep. Thus began the shelter, accommodating up to sixty people each night on the church pews. "That was probably one of the most rewarding things that has happened to me since I've been here—rewarding in terms of the ministry and rewarding in terms of the congregation. I think we all went in with some fear and trembling—as Kierkegaard titles his book—but we also went in knowing we were providing a meaningful ministry to people in the city." This program is now run by over two hundred volunteers from throughout the diocese. The "guests"—as the church calls the homeless—are welcomed by a crew of six men and women who serve them dinner, pass out blankets, and watch over them throughout the night, waking them with coffee the next morning. Peete is presently struggling with the city to obtain a permit to enable the Metrocouncil to build a permanent shelter on the church property. But until that building is completed, the homeless will be welcomed nightly at All Saints Church.

"Nan has a very sensitive awareness of the pain and struggle of all people, especially the poor and outclasses," said David I. Shoulders, member of a weekly clergy prayer group to which Peete belongs. He is particularly impressed by her "gentle, feminine way of building consensus in groups. She is a lover of all kinds of people. Her sensitivity to the hurts of minority folk is a prophetic voice for me."

"In a sense, I have two congregations," Peete explained, "the congregation I see Monday through Friday because of the feeding and outreach programs and the one I see on Sunday mornings and minister to in their homes or through hospital visits. I have hopes and expectations for both groups. I hope that, through the Metrocouncil, we will be able to build the shelter and add ancillary services such as mental health screening and preliminary job screening to help people take the next step. It's not enough just to give people food and a place to sleep! For the parish, I want to help them grow in their spiritual journeys so that liturgy becomes not just the Sunday ritual but also that which empowers them through the week to be more effective ministers in their work place and in their family lives."

The determination evident in those words is echoed in her own diocesan and national concerns. She chairs the Diocesan Urban and Social Ministries Committee and serves on the Continuing Education for Clergy Committee. Nationally, she has been appointed to the Committee for the Full Participation of Women in the Church and the Inclusive Language Subcommittee of the Standing Liturgical Commission—both groups that have required extensive time and energy. She also serves as a director of the Episcopal Church Publishing Company, which publishes *The Witness*. "She works much too hard," said one friend. "She is *driven* by all the opportunities to speak for the groups she represents—blacks, women, Episcopalians," observed another, "driven by the same need to excel that all pioneers feel: 'The whole world is watching so we have to look good!'—and she does!"

Recently, Peete and the Rev. Margaret Wood of New Zealand have been invited by the Archbishop of Canterbury to serve as consultants to the 1988 Lambeth Conference. Though she is excited by the opportunity to meet and work with Anglicans from throughout the world, she is awed by the tremendous responsibility the position entails.

Peete's home is an ur)an townhouse not far from the church. Her married daughter lives in California with a new grandchild; her son and his wife are living in a Washington, D.C., suburb. Nan and her husband continue to live separately though they have remained good friends and she has found him very supportive of her vocation. She does admit that "even though I've always combined marriage and career and children, I think as a clergywoman, I'd find it very difficult. Maybe because I don't have anyone to come home to, I work harder; but when I come home in the evening, the last thing I would really want to do is to have to cook and clean and be responsible for someone else. I am very emotionally drained at the end of most days, which for me last often until eight or nine o'clock at night. But if I had a family at home, I would maybe not work so hard and be more intentional about having a personal life."

On most days, however, Nan Peete is quite satisfied with her life as a priest. "I absolutely love what I do. I can't imagine my doing anything else or being any place else. I am like someone who is living out her fantasy, living out her dream. I am absolutely adoring that. And I feel really blessed and enriched."

Others, too, feel blessed and enriched by her ministry. "She has the gift of communication, of seeing beyond the obvious and of being able to help others see things in a fresh new way," said Nell Gibson, executive assistant to the bishop of New York. "I remember particularly a homily she delivered on what it meant to her to be able to see *one* blade of grass peeking through the sidewalk after a fire had devastated an area of Los Angeles. From the blade of grass—amidst the hopelessness and despair—she saw a glimpse of the New Jerusalem. It was a haunting analogy—one I still ponder on from time to time, when things are bleak."

Linda Gail Hornbuckle Robinson

That by the indwelling of the Holy Spirit, she may be sustained and encouraged to persevere to the end.

The Litany of Ordinations

"I had been told that women would be harder on me than men, that they would be more reluctant to accept me as a priest; but I have not experienced that to be true. I have found that women really have come to me and reached out to me simply because they trust and want my perception and my perspective. My pastoral guidance is important to them because I am a woman and have experienced life as a woman," said Linda Gail Robinson.

Deeply appreciative of the special bond she has with many women in the parish, she also admits that there are exceptions to that experience. One couple was very opposed to her coming to St. Francis Church and subsequently left the parish. "Even then, though, I had a very open and honest conversation with the wife at lunch," she said, "and we could at least talk about her objections. I didn't want them to leave. It was hard for me to let it go and accept their leaving as the choice they made. I want to fix everything and I couldn't fix that."

Robinson is the priest associate of St. Francis Church, Birmingham, Alabama. She works there about ten hours a week while she maintains a full time position as a financial planner. She preaches once a month, celebrates once a month, teaches an inquirers' class, and meets privately with several people for pastoral counseling. She fills in for the rector when he is away.

At present she does not receive pay for her work at St. Francis. She hopes that will change; she would like to be a paid assistant and wants one day to be rector of a parish. "The bishop and I made the decision that in order to find a place and a person with whom I could work very well, I would be nonstipendiary. I am not sure whether it was a fair decision, but it was a way to begin. The first agenda was to get me into a church where I could get

Linda Gail Robinson

experience as a priest and have the opportunity to give my gifts, assert my own leadership, share my skills."

Those skills are many. "Linda Gail is absolutely *real,* authentic. What you see is what she is!" said parishioner Shirley Ratliff, who serves on the diocesan department of finance. "She is able to share her deep commitment to God and her trust in him in an honest way—no cliches—just a *real* deep sharing." Her rector, Massey Gentry, is grateful for her identification with those "in any need or trouble." "Her life is the story of someone who really had to struggle in order to realize her ordination to the priesthood.

The fact that she kept at it through much difficulty and 'lives it out' is the most touching contribution she makes."

She is comfortable with her vocation. "One of the ways I approach being a woman priest is to say that, first of all, I am a priest. That is important to who I am, to my whole being. Unless someone tells me they have trouble with my being a woman, I assume that's not a problem. If they indicate there's a problem, I'll address it in a pastoral way. I can be assertive and strong about my convictions but I can also be sensitive about the difficulties those convictions may cause in another person."

What does she think women bring to the priesthood? "I hesitate to say that women are more sensitive or more nurturing or warmer; I can't separate feminine-masculine qualities that way. I think that what women bring to the religious experience is a female perspective. Men and women see the world sometimes similarly and sometimes differently. As a woman I bring the female experience, a vision shaped by how I have lived in the world. I think that sharing that viewpoint enlarges and broadens the experience of everyone."

Her most pressing difficulty is wrestling with the fact that she is not paid. She loves the parish and the opportunity to function there. She is grateful to her rector for his support. "He affirms my gifts, trusts my leadership, and has been really committed to helping the congregation see me as a priest." But the church's unreadiness to make a financial commitment to her is discouraging. "My basic feeling is that I am going to assume that what I have hoped for and worked for all my life is going to happen. I am not going to give up. I am not going to fight unnecessary battles. I am not going to back off. I am going to be there. I have a commitment to the church and I am going to hang in there! I believe with all my heart that I will be a full-time paid clergy person in the Episcopal Church some day." (Note: In January, 1988, St. Francis' vestry hired Robinson to direct an evangelism and new member outreach program. She will be compensated on a part-time basis.)

Though this present arrangement may in part be due to a more conservative stance toward women priests in the South, it was

148

primarily dictated by Robinson's family situation. She was deeply in debt when she came into the Diocese of Alabama, having borrowed to send herself through seminary and her daughter through college, while caring for her two younger sons. In addition, she had very little experience with the Episcopal Church, having entered the church only during her second year of seminary. By taking the position as a financial planner, she hoped to be able to pay off the debt quickly while gaining vocational experience in a local church.

Her path toward seminary had taken many loops and turns. As Linda Gail Herring, she grew up in Alabama as a Southern Baptist and attended Samford University in Birmingham. Married just after college, she accompanied her husband, William R. Hornbuckle, to seminary in Louisville, Kentucky, where he was trained as a Southern Baptist minister of music. Living in Alabama and Texas where he served churches, they had three children—Jennifer Lynn, Zachary and Wyn. After they moved to Fort Worth, Texas, in 1972, it became increasingly evident that their marriage was in trouble. Linda was struggling with a growing sense of vocation. She took several different positions—most in the field of social service—and began to study part time at Bright Divinity School.

In the midst of a course on women's studies that she was teaching, Linda Gail realized how important her own vocational pursuits were to her. But she and her husband found that they could not communicate on the basis of her new directions and personal growth. After several attempts to mend their marital brokenness, they were divorced in 1980.

At that point, she was working as executive director of the Southeast Area Churches, an ecumenical urban ministry in Fort Worth. A member of her board was a graduate of Yale Divinity School. At his insistence, she applied to Yale in the spring of 1981. Once accepted, "in eight weeks, I quit my job, borrowed money, put my daughter in college, leased my house, made the decisions about what furniture we would take, and moved to New Haven with my son Wyn (aged 10)." Fourteen-year-old Zachary stayed in Fort Worth with his father to finish high school.

At Yale, she discovered the Episcopal Church and was confirmed mid-way through her second year. She worked with Arthur H. Underwood, Episcopal chaplain at Yale, on a project interviewing Yale faculty about the relationship of ethics, spirituality and public policy. "She has the quality, so indispensible for a priest," said Underwood, "of an attentiveness and a listening that is both supportive and challenging. She knows how to build a community centered in Christ and calling forth the gifts of all its members."

During the summer before her final year at Yale, Linda returned to Alabama and worked for the Greater Birmingham Ministries, worshiping at the Cathedral Church of the Advent. Sponsored by that parish, she applied to Bishop Furman C. Stough for candidacy, was eventually accepted and ordained deacon in 1985. After an assignment at St. Michael and All Angels in Anniston, Alabama, she moved to St. Francis, where she was ordained priest in December, 1986.

The upheaval of this process and the weight of the responsibilities she shouldered are difficult to contemplate. A friend noted, "When Linda Gail was trying to finish her seminary work, be a mother to her children and make ends meet financially, there were times that it seemed to me she would be completely overwhelmed. On the surface, she would be ruffled and fragmented, but all the while there was a sense of her basic 'okayness' down deep. I believe that she has deep inner resources upon which to call in all kinds of crises."

In August, 1987, she married C. Andrew Robinson, a layman, chairman of the diocesan stewardship committee. "We've found a wonderful life together," she said, "though we both have very full-time careers and he has three children and I have three children and we are both very involved in the church. If we can continue to sit down and talk about the demands and the hopes of our lives, we will be tremendous support to each other. It is exciting to share my life and my ministry and his life and his career."

Fran Toy

All baptized people are called to make Christ known as Savior and Lord, and to share in the renewing of his world. Now you are called to work as a pastor, priest, and teacher, together with your bishop and fellow presbyters, and to take your share in the councils of the church.

The Examination

"It was on a free afternoon at a church conference after I had returned to my room that I very clearly felt God saying to me, 'Where have you been all these years? I've been waiting for you.' I was forty-three years old. My two children would be in college shortly. My husband and I were looking forward to having an empty nest, doing some traveling, retiring eventually and growing old gracefully."

Fran Toy is Chinese-American, third generation Californian. Her childhood was a blend of two cultures. Though the neighborhood was largely Asian, the public schools included children of other ethnic backgrounds. After school, she and her siblings spent two more hours each day at Chinese school. Within her family, the traditional Chinese culture held sway—the centrality of family life, respect for elders, and obedience to authority were learned at an early age.

The Episcopal Church was an important part of that life. Her parents had met and married at the True Sunshine Episcopal Church, an ethnic mission begun when the Oakland Chinese community was established just after the 1906 earthquake. Her mother continued to be actively involved in that congregation. Fran taught Sunday School, participated in the Girls' Friendly Society and the Young People's Fellowship, played the piano for the choir, and even—with her brother and sister—cleaned the church building each week.

After graduation from the University of California, Fran married Arthur Chun Toy and the couple moved in with his parents above

Fran Toy

their grocery store and lived there with Art's brother, wife, and two children and another sister. The entire family ate dinners together, the mother cooking and the three younger women cleaning up afterward. Fran taught kindergarten for two years, then resigned to care for daughter Tami, born in 1959, and son Glen, born in 1961. When Glen started school, she returned to teaching and the family moved into a home of their own.

Toy's life was full and happy—she had work she loved, her own home, children growing and prospering. At the Church of Our Savior (which True Sunshine Church had chosen as its new name), she had plunged into church life—lay reader, chalice bearer, senior warden, deputy to diocesan convention. "Why me? Why now?" she thought to herself in 1977 when God's call came with such clarity.

She had felt God's call once before, as a teenager, but put it out of her mind as she grew up. But the urgency of the second experience would not be denied. After discussions with her family, her local priest, Victor T. Wei, and male and female clergy whom Wei recommended that she talk with, Toy applied for postulancy. "I had promised to finance my children's college education first," Toy said, "so I taught half time and began course work at the Church Divinity School of the Pacific. It took me five years to complete seminary."

In 1985, two months before her fifty-first birthday, Fran Toy was ordained, the Episcopal Church's first Asian-American woman priest. Two years later, she was hired as the coordinator of alumni/ ae affairs at the Church Divinity School of the Pacific. With an office at the seminary, she is charged with maintaining information about the alumns, working with the Alumni/ae Council to plan events and projects, traveling to various areas to develop alumni/ ae networks in those areas, and answering correspondence about the deployment of CDSP graduates. The position is part time.

"Of the seven people we interviewed for the position, we had no doubt that Fran was the most qualified," said Richard K. Toll, Alumni/ae Association president. "In her years of work as a laywoman and as a priest, she had developed a strong community attitude about the seminary. She knew the diocese. And she is a very organized person—that came through in all her materials."

One of the advantages Toy brings to this position is high visibility. As the only Asian-American woman priest, she has been asked to serve on several national committees, including the Presiding Bishop's Task Force on Women's Full Participation in the Church. She had served as a national board member of the Episcopal Women's Caucus and now serves on the board of directors of the Episcopal Women's History Project. She devotes much energy and time to these volunteer groups out of a strong sense of personal responsibility. "It's important that people see a different model of ministry," she said. "I've experienced racism and sexism, so my words about those issues carry experiential validity."

Toy's present task is to try to meet with as many of the seminary graduates as possible to devise better ways of maintaining a mutual relationship. She extends her trips to national board meetings to include alumni gatherings in the area.

One of the long range goals of CDSP is to develop better relations with, and understandings of, the Asian cultures of the Pacific Rim. The advantage of having Toy as an ambassador for the seminary is obvious. "I have always seen myself as a bridge person. It is a gift to me that because my mother was trained as a teacher in China, we spoke pure Cantonese in our home. Church services were all in Chinese when I grew up. All the canticles were sung, all the hymns were sung in Chinese. And although I lost a lot of it, when I went to church in Hong Kong as an adult and they were singing the *Venite,* it all came back."

Before her appointment at CDSP, Toy served as an interim pastor at the original True Sunshine Church in San Francisco, where she preached and celebrated in both Chinese and English. She later had two other interim assignments. "Her evident spirituality and a cheerful, no-nonsense directness about getting the task done was very helpful to our parish," said Dr. Jeptha Boone, senior warden of Christ Church, Alameda. "The response to her was very favorable—several long-term antagonists to women in the clergy were won over."

Gary Lawrence described the way Toy operated at the Church of the Resurrection, Pleasant Hill: "She showed respect and honor to me as senior warden. This caused me to be more the senior warden who deserved respect and honor. She did the same for others in our parish and thereby called forth our ministries in positive ways."

The altar at that church had been raised on blocks for the previous rector who was over six feet tall. Toy, at four feet, eleven inches, had at first wanted to have the blocks removed, but then decided that because she was temporary, it would be wiser to accommodate herself to the altar as it was. "Seeing her small self behind that great altar was inspiring. She adjusted to the church's needs and was happy to do so," said Lawrence.

Accommodation, respect, honor, gentleness, competence—these are qualities that Fran Toy brings to the priesthood. People who work with her quickly recognize her extraordinary skill as a bridge-builder, as a reconciler. Her ease of manner, her warm humor and her zest for life all convey to those who know her the reality of God's "good news" for the world.

Janet C. Watrous with Cathy Brennan, a student at St. Mary's

Janet C. Watrous

You are to love and serve the people among whom you work, caring alike for young and old, strong and weak, rich and poor.

The Examination

Imagine being priest to a parish made up of five hundred young women between the ages of sixteen and twenty who are required to attend church each week. How does one deal with the mood swings of late adolescence as well as the problems that beset young adults? How does one establish an atmosphere of openness and approachability, the ability to "be there" for counsel when a young woman's world has just collapsed, and at the same time oversee the myriad details of regular services and academic schedules?

Place the congregation in the midst of a lovely wooded campus in Raleigh, North Carolina, and you have the setting for Janet Watrous' ministry. She serves as chaplain of St. Mary's College, the only Episcopal high school and college for women. The four-year school offers the last two years of high school and first two years of college. Watrous' responsibilities include planning worship services, counseling students, faculty and staff, maintaining connections between the college and the five surrounding dioceses, and working with various academic and diocesan boards and committees.

Central to campus life is the chapel with services scheduled three days a week and Sunday morning. "We are an old-fashioned school," Watrous explained, "in that we still require chapel attendance for the students. While students are here, the chapel is their church home. They act as layreaders and chalice bearers and serve as members of the vestry. I hope that what each student learns here about being a responsible member of the body of Christ will be a continuing aspect of her religious life."

"One of my greatest challenges is to try to get young women to be more realistic about the possible choices for their lives," she said. "I used to think that would just come from growing up; but I can see now that it doesn't *just happen*. One needs to have catalysts—teachers, priests, just friends—to help produce that kind of growth. There are lots of women today who have been "girls" all their lives. So I'm trying to be that kind of catalytic force without offending, without sounding like I'm putting them down, without being a know-it-all."

She works hard at that task, urging students to voice the unasked questions about their futures. Through casual remarks to chapel volunteers or chance conversations at lunch, Watrous tries to stretch the students' vistas, to empower them to take charge of their own lives. "I ask them what they would like to be doing in the year 2000. And then we talk about some of the choices it would take to get there."

Also on her agenda as chaplain is leading young women to grapple with the meaning of Christianity in their lives. She brings in women speakers who are willing to talk about their own faith. She offers a spiritual gifts workshop during which students attempt to identify their talents. "We talk about human skills as being gifts from God. And ask, what do your gifts tell you about what God is doing in your life? What might a person as gifted as you are do with her life in response to God's gifts? What do you think God wants you to do?"

In addition to campus work, Watrous has an extensive schedule of speaking throughout the diocese for St. Mary's College. "Most of my talks have been with Episcopal Church Women," she said. "I cannot overemphasize how important their support has been to me. They reached out to me even before I arrived. The Commission on Women's Issues even paid the air fare so that I could be interviewed for this position! They were committed to having a woman priest as chaplain and since then, have been open and caring and interested in hearing my story. Their encouragement has been crucial to my feeling at home here."

When Watrous applied for the position in 1985, the school's search committee had narrowed the list of candidates to five men. However, they did arrange to interview Janet. Putting aside her misgivings about being a northerner, a woman and a nonacademic and buoyed by the support of the Commission on Women's Issues, Watrous flew to Raleigh. "The interview went extremely well. I knew almost instantly that this was the place for me and I felt the warm approval of many of the committee members." In a matter of weeks she had been offered and had accepted the position.

The move was a major transition for the family. Janet and her husband, Robert C. Kochersberger, had a son Charles, six, and a daughter Anne, four. They were living in Cortland, New York, where Robert taught journalism at State University. For him, the move meant leaving a tenured position as associate professor to begin a job search in North Carolina. He now teaches at North Carolina State University, but only on a temporary appointment.

The problem of balancing two careers is one of the most difficult tasks married clergywomen and their husbands face. "This has been a source of *great conflict* in our relationship," Watrous admitted, "because in a marriage when the power shifts—not in your own sense but in the world's sense—when the wife is perceived as being so powerful that she can make her husband move, then no matter how much you say, 'Well, our relationship isn't like that,' it's very tough not to buy into what the world says."

She recognizes that her husband effectively put his career on hold in order to make the move, to a situation where she held the high status position. Since they moved into a house on campus, their every day living is also within *her* social space. "My husband does not get a lot of psychological support for the really significant sacrifice in terms of his career that he made," Watrous said.

How do they deal with the tension associated with these changes? They try to talk about it honestly with each other. They are developing friendships with people at St. Mark's Church, where Bob and the children are members, and they try to make summers special family times to get away from the campus and the fishbowl existence there. They have seen the tension as part of the give-and-take of any marriage. In that spirit, Janet declares that in all probability, their next move will be determined by Bob's career demands.

What has ordination meant to Janet Watrous? "My whole adult life has been growing up with this issue," she said. "My call to the vocation of priest has defined my life. To pursue that vocation has meant being involved in history." The call came to her during her senior year at college at the University of East Anglia, Norwich, England. Two years' study in England had given her a wider view of the world while stimulating questions about her place in that world. Her approaching graduation and possible career opportunities were much on her mind when in the midst of a church service, "It suddenly came to me, clear as a bell, 'Go to seminary.' I have had only two experiences where I really felt that God was speaking to me. That day was one. There was no question to me but that I was being directed."

She returned home and enrolled at the Episcopal Divinity School in Cambridge, Massachusetts, in September, 1972. When Watrous entered, there were three other women in her class and only ten in the student body. She left after her second year, worked for two years, and returned to graduate in 1977.

Why did she leave? "I attended the Louisville General Convention the fall of my second year, knowing that women's ordination was due to be voted upon. At that point I really did not know much about the church—its political structure, how things got done. Louisville opened my eyes. The discord was unbelievable! While there, I was introduced as a seminary student to one man who blatantly refused to shake hands with me. I had never met personal rejection like that. And then there was that horrible moment when the motion for women's ordination was defeated. It was like dying! With extraordinary clarity I realized that I was one small part of a huge, terribly significant issue—there was far more at stake here than my own self-discovery. God was either doing something very wonderful in this world or else something awful was happening. That sense of cataclysmic change and forboding followed me back to seminary, casting a gloom over the rest of the year. I concluded that I could not cope with having my whole life wrapped around that issue. I felt lost, alone, scared. So I left school and worked for the next two years with a prisoner rehabilitation program. However, I also applied for, and received, candidacy from the Diocese of Central New York."

Not only was the work therapeutic, providing Watrous with a sense of her own capabilities and administrative skills, but the change of location brought many new friends. She met and fell in love with Robert Kochersberger. They were engaged to be married when she returned to seminary for her final year.

In the fall of 1976, everything fell into place. The academic work was challenging and stimulating; the seminary community became a source of strength. General Convention approved the ordination of women to the priesthood—an event that offered reality to Janet's long-held dream. She was accepted by the Diocese of Central New York as a candidate for holy orders. In May she and Robert were married. In June she graduated and was ordained deacon by Bishop Ned Cole and went directly to work as an assistant pastor at the Tabernacle United Methodist Church in Binghamton, New York, since no jobs were available in local Episcopal churches. Having had women ministers for many years, the Methodists were not threatened by Janet's ministry. She found challenges and approval within that setting. At the end of the year, she was ordained priest at Tabernacle Church.

Though her bishop was personally very supportive, he found few congregations ready to call a woman priest. For the next six years, Janet served as an interim pastor in five different congregations. She and her husband (with son Charles, who was born in 1979) moved to Cortland, New York, where he had a teaching position at State University. Janet served as priest-in-charge at Grace Church, Cortland, for a year, then at Grace Church, Waverly, and Christ Church, Wellsburg—two congregations fifteen miles apart—a sixty-mile drive from Cortland. Daughter Anne was born just before the second assignment. The family moved for a year to Knoxville, Tennessee, where Robert worked on his doctorate while Janet served another interim stint at St. Francis' Church, Norris. Then back to Cortland and SUNY and another interim position.

The pressures on the young couple were great. There were the difficulty of trying to adjust family patterns to two careers, the demands of two small children, and a job that required mother to drive sixty miles to work. And as a pioneer, Watrous was shaping a ministry for which she had few role models. Yet, with each new congregation, she was more convinced of the rightness of her choice of profession.

"Most of all, I have asked very little of the church," she said. "I have been underpaid and overtraveled. The institutional church was not at all prepared to relate in a supportive way to me, a young wife, mother and priest. Thankfully, the support of congregations made me feel really appreciated. I believe that the vocational reality has got to be the binding one—the knowledge that God does not let you down. While I've only been a young woman in all of this, I have faced tremendous isolation and loneliness. Nothing prepared me for that. But it made me see that the authenticity of my call is always upheld by God, even when the institutional church is stumbling. My relationship with the *people* in the church has been so powerful, so satisfying, that I have been able to do more, and stretch higher, than I had ever dreamed possible. That relationship inspires and sustains me but the primary relationship is between myself and God.''

Colleagues comment on her strength and hard work, tempered with compassion and "willingness to look at all sides of an issue." Even her weaknesses are strengths, said Marcia Jones, St. Mary's former dean of students: "She won't give up, so some would call her stubborn; I would call her strong. She also wanted change, was discontent to accept things just because of 'tradition.' Some would say she lacked patience. I would say she has courage and determination."

Her self-assurance enables her to share her gifts with others. "She has been a real friend and ministered to me," said one co-worker. "She deepened my appreciation of liturgy and made me more impatient with some of the language that is no longer appropriate," said another. She is gradually developing for herself a role within the diocese as a supporter of women's initiatives and a builder of female networks of support. Janet Watrous has moved into the second decade of her own ordination with assurance and grace.

Geralyn Wolf

For a blessing upon all human labor, and for the right use of the riches of creation, that the world may be freed from poverty, famine, and disaster, we pray to you, O Lord.

The Litany for Ordinations

"In February, 1987, I began my new ministry as dean of Christ Church Cathedral, Louisville, Kentucky. The media coverage was extensive, bringing to mind how few people were interested in me as a mission priest, but how many were interested in the phenomenon of a woman dean. In some ways it lifted up the weaknesses of a society and church that gave more attention to titles than to works of ministry. Though I recognize the importance of my position for all women, the lack of attention paid to our inner cities and the ministry there is painful," commented Geralyn Wolf.

Wolf is the first woman priest to be elected dean. Christ Church Cathedral is located downtown, in the midst of a commercial area. Without a residential locus, the cathedral draws parishioners from all parts of the city. Many loyal members pass two or three Episcopal churches on their drive to Sunday morning services.

When she arrived in Louisville, Wolf realized that the widespread nature of her flock needed to be addressed. Her first priority was strengthening the sense of community among the members. Worship was central to this task. "The first thing that I did was to move the altar. Where once we were using a high altar, facing east, we now have a free-standing altar which, I think, is a crucial step for bringing a scattered people into a gathered community," explained Wolf. "Then, with the help of organist Mark Johnson, we concentrated on the music, choosing settings for the Eucharist that lend themselves to congregational singing. We try to use just one setting each season, going over the music at the beginning of the first Sunday's service and teaching it in adult class. Singing draws people together."

Along with the worship, Wolf proceeded to strengthen adult education. The format had relied primarily on visiting speakers on a variety of topics. Instead, Wolf assumed leadership of that class. "I needed to get to know the people and they needed to get to know me in a way that wasn't possible in the Sunday Eucharists. I also felt as though we needed to know from whence we had come and that the Exodus story was the story of all of us who are on a pilgrimage of faith. So I talked about Moses and the Exodus and the other people who were part of that story. Then I shared my own journey of faith. Now we have broken into groups and one Sunday a month the groups meet separately and one member of each group shares his or her own journey of faith." On the other three Sundays, the class is focusing on what it means to be a Christian, to be one of Christ's disciples.

A disciplined spiritual life is central to Gerry Wolf's understanding of the ministry and she has worked to share this concept with her congregation. Morning Prayer is read each day in the cathedral.

Midweek Eucharists are offered on Monday and Wednesday evenings. "Chairs are placed in a semicircle around the altar. It is important for us to be close to each other in the presence of God. I write the intercessions now, drawing the lessons, the concerns of our world and city, and personal needs together. There is time for individual response, and always the silence, so necessary for our listening," she explained. "The other night we had our first 'quiet evening' where we just came together for three hours to be silent, reflect on some passages of scripture, some meditations. It was very special, thirty of us sitting quietly together, seeking God."

Finding strength in communal religious life has been a consistent experience for Wolf. After graduating from West Chester University in Philadelphia, she taught for four years at George School and lived in the midst of the Quaker community there. In 1974 she entered the Episcopal Divinity School in Cambridge, Massachusetts. Instead of living at the seminary, however, she stayed at the convent of the Society of St. Margaret and gained from the sisters "my continued devotion to the religious life." She also spent three weeks at the Taize Community in France during that period.

When she graduated from seminary, she returned to the Diocese of Pennsylvania where she was ordained and served as an assistant at two parishes. In 1981 she was appointed vicar of St. Mary's Church, a small, predominantly black, parish in urban Philadelphia. The church had been without a vicar for ten years and had even been marked for closing at one point. However, with Wolf's arrival, it got a new lease on life. She had three guiding principles: "to use every available resource—people, programs, property; to assess the needs of the neighborhood and connect them with resources to meet those needs; and to make decisions that would benefit the community rather than particular individuals." Using that strategy, the church began a soup kitchen, a food cooperative, a thrift shop, and a reading program. They extended the ministry to whites who were moving into the area as the process of urban "gentrification" proceeded.

Just next door (sharing a common brick wall) to the rectory where Wolf lived was a dilapidated building the parish owned.

With some parishioners, Wolf decided to renovate that building for communal living, which they did with help from professional contractors when necessary. Bainbridge House became the site for an experiment in urban communal living. The men and women who lived there committed themselves to a shared prayer life and ministry to the neighborhood. They ate their meals together, using a different cook each night. "It was a bit odd in today's world for people to come together to live that kind of life—a group of people all about the same age who each said 'this is the way I would like to live.' We didn't do any of those things that could be connected with Anglican orders. We just decided that we would like to serve Jesus in that particular neighborhood and it was easier for us to do that together than alone," Wolf explained.

The depth of Wolf's ministry at St. Mary's was what caught the eyes of members of the cathedral who were searching for a new dean. Louisville's former dean, Allen L. Bartlett Jr., had been elected bishop coadjutor of Pennsylvania. Several cathedral members had met Wolf when they went to Philadelphia for Bartlett's consecration, which she coordinated. Later, when her name appeared among the candidates for dean, committee members remembered her efficient work at the consecration. The group who traveled to Philadelphia to interview her were particularly impressed with the outreach program at St. Mary's Church and by the high esteem in which Wolf was held in the diocese for her organizing skills and liturgical expertise.

After the list of candidates had been narrowed to five, Wolf was invited to Louisville to meet the cathedral chapter and the search committee. "That interview clinched it," said Lawrence Otto, the present senior warden. "There was just absolute electricity in the room—something was going on. I like to think the Holy Spirit was at work, but whatever, it was really almost mystical. It felt *right.*"

Having a woman as dean has not pleased everyone, particularly some of the older women. One parishioner said, "Gerry has a way about her that has been difficult for a lot of people in that she is very straightforward, very upfront, has no hidden agenda—but she can be very blunt about things. She's a person who really knows where she is in regard to her own personhood." In addition, there are people who feel that the pastoral areas—particularly calling in the homes—are being neglected. Wolf is frank to say that the demands of the new position have left her little time for pastoral visiting and she needs assistance in this area. The cathedral is planning to hire a canon with strong pastoral skills to complement her ministry.

Wolf continues to work at building the kind of networks that will strengthen the parish fabric. She's had a series of open houses at the deanery, inviting everyone to join in a potluck meal. She's visited with people during neighborhood coffees, organized by zip codes, and has been invited to dinners, parties and family gatherings. "I found then our members are all over the city," she laughed. She bought a house in an older section of the city—an area of lower and middle income people, black and white. The house is divided into apartments; she lives in one and rents the others. In a sense, her neighborhood is a microcosm of the city.

What is the ministry that Christ Church Cathedral must have to the city of Louisville? Wolf doesn't yet know. "I haven't done anything with the city. For me, I need to figure out what is going on at home base before going out. I think my primary obligation is always to the parish which I serve, then to the other groups. Above all, the job description of any priest ought to be to preach, to teach, and to bring the sacramental life into the community as a reality. Each of us must have the patience to wait to see what grows out of that life, and not be afraid to be transformed by it."

David, Priscilla, Stewart and John Wood

Priscilla Peacock Wood

For her family, that they may be adorned with all Christian virtues, we pray to you, O Lord.

The Litany for Ordinations

"Generally I am thought of as a priest. The fact that I am female has not made a great deal of difference to the vast majority of people that I have been with. I have always thought that I'd like less emphasis put on the fact that I'm a woman priest. I am a priest and never mind what sex I am, just let me get on with doing that ministry—doing what God has called on me to do."

Wife, mother, priest, rector—Priscilla Wood is one of the growing number of women priests who combine a full-time position with the responsibilities of raising a family. Her vocation has been a family affair from the beginning. Married three months before she entered General Theological Seminary, the Woods moved to New York in 1976. Husband Stewart took a teaching position to provide financial support, assisted with household tasks and typed Priscilla's papers. Midway through the second year, their first child, David, was born. Aided by faculty members who were willing to be flexible about assignment deadlines and class schedules, Priscilla finished the next two years. "With his lunch box in hand, David went off to the seminary day-care facility at the age of seven months and we have pictures of him doing that. Now at the ripe old age of nine, he looks back at that with a giggling sort of pride," she recounted.

After ordination, Priscilla worked as curate at St. Paul's Church in Morris Plains, New Jersey, while Stewart taught school nearby. Their second son was born there. "That parish had had a woman curate before but not a pregnant priest. I found being pregnant to be no more burdensome than it would have been if I had been teaching school or working as an attorney. It did, however, at the end get a little crowded around the altar rail because the space between the altar and rail was a bit narrow. But that only served to give the rector—David Hamilton—and me a few good laughs! As far as I could see, no one in the parish was upset or bothered about my condition."

"Being married and having a career and a family is right for me. I know that I am not called to stay home and raise children without working outside the home. I think the fact that the boys now (they are nine and six) find it so easy to get aong with different people is in part because from the time that they were a few weeks old, they have for part of each day been in the care of someone else. We have had a variety of arrangements for child care, from pre-school and day-care situations to a series of live-in nannies," she said.

Wood is rector of St. James Church in Piqua, Ohio, a position she has held since 1985. St. James is a small (65 pledging units), stable parish, the only Episcopal Church in the community. As such, it is a social center for the congregation and maintains an active program of worship, Christian education, parish meetings and ministry to the sick and the elderly.

Sunday Eucharists are at eight and ten, with church school for all ages at nine. Planning the worship is a team ministry for the Woods because Stewart serves as the organist. "We really enjoy working together at this. It is something that we have wanted to do for a long time," she said. "When we got here, there was an adult choir that was mostly men. Gradually, Stewart has been able to recruit a few more women for the adult choir, and has organized a carol choir of non-readers and a family choir of the older children and their parents."

During the week, Wood spends a great deal of time visiting shut-ins and those who are in the hospital. "One of the things the parish wanted very much was somebody who would make those kinds of pastoral contacts and visits. I enjoy doing that very much." Many of her parishioners have commented on how much they appreciate that ministry.

Wood enjoys less the administrative duties, particularly committee meetings. Each member of the vestry chairs a committee, such as stewardship or Christian education, and Wood tries to be available for each meeting. "I keep some sense of perspective," she said, "by remembering my field work supervisor's statement that administration is a ministry. To organize good agendas and have fast-moving committee meetings that make decisions is, in its own way, pastoral to those people with whom you are working."

The vestry plans a capital fund drive to raise $200,000 for a major rehabilitation of the church building. The structure is almost ninety years old. While it has been well-maintained, the roof needs extensive repairs and the stained glass windows need to be cleaned and reset. In addition, they hope to install an elevator for the increasing number of older parishioners and provide a small endowment for future work. "My overall intention is to work on stewardship so that more and more of our money can go out beyond the parish," Wood explained. "Having a major fund drive and getting some of those big projects finished will give the parish a sense of accomplishment and the chance to start looking beyond themselves."

She also wants to focus on evangelism. "There are a lot of unchurched people in this community and we should be reaching out to them. And also, there are a number of people on our list who consider themselves Episcopalians but never darken the doors of the church. We need to reach these lapsed members."

Has Wood been effective in initiating these programs? One vestrywoman who originally did not think that St. James would be receptive to a woman priest has been impressed with Wood's "sincerity about her faith and her calling and her total involvement in *all* facets of parish life. Church members appreciate her hard work. Church attendance is on the rise," she said, while admitting that "we lost several old ladies from the congregation at the beginning and they have not yet returned."

Another woman, Bonnie Shullenberger, asked to describe Wood's ministry, answered: "Priscilla is strong, stubborn, faithful, orthodox, progressive, direct, patient, courteous, careful, and maternal. You don't have enough time for me to elaborate on all these qualities."

What are the personal rewards Wood finds in being a priest? "Most exciting and wonderful to me is that special relationship that you build up with people as you share with them their most open and intimate times—baptism, marriage, the death of loved ones. If you are careful and gentle and loving and God is with you, that can be a very rewarding and special time. I think baptisms are the most exciting and enjoyable thing that I do. Funerals I find in many ways enriching and intimate because that is often a particularly raw and open time with people. Weddings are fun but more often than not, I get frustrated with the couple because they are so ready and willing to focus on the *wedding* but they don't really want to pay much attention to the *marriage.*"

Wood is beginning to make friends with whom she can relax and play. She gets strong support for her ministry from her husband and family. "One of the things that Stewart and I have tried to work very hard at doing is to schedule in family time— time with the boys and time with just the two of us—almost the same way that we schedule any of the other events in our lives. Stewart teaches high school math and extra courses at the junior college here, as well as directing the choirs. In addition, we've just bought an 1870 house with a big yard. The maintenance and yard work take time. So our lives are very full and wonderful," she said.

One missing element, however, is a supportive relationship with other clergy. "When I was in Bronxville, I met for lunch once a month with four other clergy. When we began meeting, we were all curates in our second curacies, and looking toward the possibility of being rectors. So we called ourselves the curates *emeriti*. The spiritual guidance and freedom to talk about knotty problems with my colleagues was very important to me. I have tried to make the kind of connections here that would duplicate that kind of support but so far it has been impossible. A neighboring priest and I had just begun to meet, and now he has been called to another diocese. I will have to try again."

Does she think her ministry is different because she is a woman? "I don't really know how to answer that. Perhaps some of us bring a different slant on things, being traditionally nurturing. And yet, I know that, on the whole, men who go into the priesthood are very nurturing and pastoral. And women, who are thought not to have great administrative skills, have long been able to administer complex households. It's a matter of realizing that everybody, whether male or female, has different strengths and gifts. To put away half the human race and bottle up and not use their many gifts because they are women is foolish."

Women priests—the effect

What have women priests meant to the life of the Episcopal Church? "Enrichment, tremendous enrichment," said Sam Hulsey, bishop of Northwest Texas. "Many more gifts are held up in terms of modeling and sharing. It's meant the opening up of ministry in exciting ways."

"It was by women clergy that I was taught the ministry of the baptized," said Sandol Stoddard, a laywoman from Hawaii. "I gained a new sense of responsibility as a Christian and a kind of *nerve* that no male clergyman had encouraged in me. The presence of women clergy topples the false notions of male hierarchical power that have interfered with our perception of true Christian values for too long."

"We do not fully recognize nor appreciate yet the added dimension that women bring," contended the Reverend Victor T. Wei, executive officer of the Diocese of California. "It is not so much that they bring the feminine (men can do that) but that collective constellation of womanhood—some concrete and some intangible—which continues to interact with the Spirit and the Church."

"A visitor to my parish came to me in tears after a service in which she had received communion from a woman priest. She said it was the first time she had felt so deeply connected to the worship of the church as a woman. She felt whole and good about herself," said Scott Kallstrom, vicar of Grace Van Vorst Church in Jersey City, New Jersey.

"This is an issue that has been very painful for people on both sides," cautioned William C. Wantland, bishop of Eau Claire. "In my diocese, I would have to say that probably somewhere between two-thirds and three-fourths of the overall communicant strength would have some problems with women's ordination."

"I just feel that a woman's theology is different and it's more like my theology," explained Elvira Charles, a laywoman from Massachusetts. "I'm not clear why that is so but I have a sense of being included when I hear her speak. It's as though she is talking *my* language and that's nurturing because so much of the religious experience is other than that for me."

Obviously any assessment of the effect of women priests must be largely subjective, filtered through individual understanding of the nature of the church and perception of the activities of the people of God. While it is apparent that there is widespread popular support for women priests, some significant problems remain.

Most perplexing is the situation of many dedicated church members who continue to be opposed to the ordination of women. The following thoughtful statement from Donald J. Parsons, recently retired bishop of Quincy, highlights some of the concerns of these Episcopalians:

"Advocates of the ordination of women rejoice at the actions of the Episcopal Church in giving permission for such a change. With a mixture of regret and resignation, and perhaps a dash of relief, Episcopalians have seen some clergy and laity leave this Church for other Christian families. The number of such departures has not been overwhelming, which may unfortunately conceal the loss we have incurred. Those departing were dedicated and active communicants. Many will feel their dedication was narrow or misdirected, but these Church members were not among the apathetic. The loss of their fervor is not a trivial matter.

"Yet even more important is the effect of this great change on many, both lay and clerical, who cannot in conscience accept this departure from ancient tradition and who have remained in the Episcopal fold. It is impossible to estimate their number, but it is much too easy to forget their existence. For various reasons they cannot agree with what they see as an innovation which is theologically wrong and/or a grave stumbling-block in the path of Church reunion. They remain as Episcopalians, but what is their lot? Increasingly they find themselves in a most unhappy position. The majority of Episcopalians believe the issue is settled, and they are impatient with those who feel their conscientious resistance is now merely resented. Many of them feel betrayed, as what was passed by General Convention as permissive is now claimed to be mandated. In 1976 the emphasis was on being open to what the Holy Spirit would say to the Church. Now such openness appears to be forbidden. Then we heard a lot about Gamaliel in Acts 5:38-39, but now he has been again relegated to his former obscurity.

"Such conscientious objectors are troublesome to the majority, but it is painful indeed to find oneself accused of breaking the law, when the law was only a permissive one. Worse still, such persons are in a sense excommunicated if a diocesan or other area Eucharist includes women priests as concelebrants. There is an increasing fear that the little bit of tolerance still allowed will in the future be given a time-limit. As one bishop poignantly expressed it, 'How can I be sure I'll die before that time-limit is reached?' A major change will inevitably produce some casualties, but it is false history to overlook or deny their existence. The price is paid by the Church as caring laity and clergy leave their Episcopal home, but as others remain in their Church but are made to feel they are unwanted and even resented, they also pay a price."

Bishop Parsons' statement indicates the pain and ambivalence which many of those Episcopalians opposed to ordaining women priests continue to feel. However, the strong Anglican tradition of toleration for opposing viewpoints has encouraged communicants on both sides of the issue to work at continuing the dialogue within a church whose official political structure has affirmed priesthood for women. To date, most who are opposed to priesthood for women have chosen to remain within the Episcopal Church. And most Episcopalians who endorse priesthood for women have hesitated to push for any official political action to force the issue in dioceses which have opposed it.

As Bishop Parsons suggests, however, there is a question as to how long this "truce of toleration" will continue. The essential commitment of the Christian gospel to the equality of all persons before God was seen by many people as the compelling reason to end the exclusion of women from the priesthood and the episcopate. Those who argue on this basis of equality find it difficult to accept continuing inequality for women, even if only in a few dioceses.

Furthermore, the women priests themselves are cruelly caught in the ambivalence of the church's stance. Each woman priest knows that her priesthood was validated by the church at her ordination. When she meets church members who conscientiously refuse to accept that validation, she can't help but ask, "What does it mean to be a member of a church? Does it not mean that you accept that church's Constitution and Canons? Does it not mean that you recognize that church's priesthood?" As Sandra Horton, assistant at St. David's Church, Roswell, Georgia, explained, "As an ordained woman, I am prohibited by a number of bishops from exercising any sacramental ministry in their diocese, even as a visitor. In any diocese, a male priest may exercise his sacerdotal ministry at the invitation of another priest; however, in several dioceses, a woman must have permission of the bishop. We've still got a long way to go!"

The "conscience clause" and its ramifications continues to be a source of tension, but this has been a tension with which the church has been able to live. The ties of unity have proved stronger than those of division.

A second continuing problem is that of the deployment of women priests. Though today it generally is possible for women to find initial placements as assistants after finishing seminary, it is difficult for clergywomen to move from being an assistant to being in charge of a parish. As was demonstrated earlier, far more men than women priests ordained since 1977 are in charge of parishes.

To confront this problem, several bishops or diocesan councils have begun to require search committees to interview both men and women candidates. Often such interviews have resulted in a woman's being called as rector. Women priests also are becoming more sophisticated about working within the church's deployment system by watching for advertised vacancies and applying for those positions. A consortium of organizations has established a monthly newsletter, O.P.E.N., which lists vacant positions and provides helpful information about job-hunting.

Many clergywomen have limited their placement opportunities by choosing to stay in a specific location because of a husband's employment or the children's advantageous school situation. Though they would own the fact that the decision was theirs to make, these women often admit to a sense of frustration at not being able to explore fully their own potential for leadership. Generally, however, they are also quick to point out that this is a frustration they share with other married professional women.

Allied to the question of deployment is that of salary. Although no national study has compared the salaries of men and women priests, there is evidence of financial discrimination. When John H. Morgan surveyed three-hundred-fifty Episcopal women priests on a wide range of issues, thirty-five per cent of the women answered "no" to the question, "Is your financial compensation fair?"[1] Often there is little financial discrimination in a clergywoman's initial placement which tends to be under diocesan regulation of minimum salaries. However, in the second and third jobs in parishes that have some flexibility in setting salaries, inequities begin to appear.

In addition, a number of women have been willing to accept positions at less than adequate compensation, with the promise that "once the parish gets back on its feet," their wages will increase. Often, the mechanisms for enforcing that kind of promise have proved ineffective. Some might agree to work for a regular salary but without benefits such as pension and medical insurance because they receive those benefits from their husbands' employers.

Ultimately the question of adequate financial compensation must be the responsibility of the clergywoman herself. With diocesan awareness of possible pitfalls and a sensitivity on the part of vestry members, contracts can be negotiated that are fair and equitable.

A more complex issue is that of power and authority within the church. Women priests are making a way for themselves within a hierarchy that is still dominated by men. They find themselves asking how they can live comfortably within that hierarchy while setting strategies to shift its power base. Most clergywomen admit that their first few years after ordination are spent shaping their own ministries and simply seeking to survive in a man's world. But as the number of clergywomen has grown, and a cadre of experienced, successful women priests has developed, the commitment to form women's networks of support and communication is emerging. Whether such networks will attack the hierarchical model itself or simply promote women to positions of importance within the hierarchy is yet to be seen.

Despite these difficulties, the benefits of opening the priesthood and the episcopate to women have been significant to the Episcopal Church. The pastoral ministry to women has been enhanced as women priests speak and act from their own experience about the issues that confront women. Premarital counseling takes on a new dimension when a couple is able to speak of their upcoming marriage with both male and female priests. Husbands and wives both find that women priests often bring a different experience to counseling on issues of marriage and family life. Women dealing with difficult pregnancies and childbirth are comforted by the presence of pastors who are themselves mothers.

Women, young and old, find role models among the clergywomen, building a spiritual life of their own as they emulate a particular woman priest. The sense that religion can be an important reality in women's lives as well as men's lives is symbolized for children in the presence of women in the sanctuary. "I have felt the deepest personal satisfaction and fulfillment in my own life in the Church to see women representing me and all women in the sacramental life of the Church. I did not know how much I had missed this until I experienced the difference," wrote one grandmother.

Role modeling works for men, too, who experience with women priests the opportunity to express the feminine side of their own nature and to admit their own vulnerability. "When my husband discovered his cancer had metastasized," revealed one woman, "he went to our priest, with whom he was able to cry and talk of his despair about his prospects and about God and faith. She permitted this outpouring as well as offering comfort, helping him to reexamine his faith and gather strength for the next round of treatment options. He is very clear that he could not have taken all these emotions and doubts and anger to any male priests we know."

Women priests bring a new dimension to clergy gatherings. "I *like* being with the women as peers," said David I. Shoulders, canon to the ordinary in the Diocese of Indianapolis. "I think an all-male clericus is *boring!* For too long the church has been without the relational emphasis, the gentleness, the skillful sensitivity, and the peculiar competencies of women. What a wonderful refreshing change all of us are going through because of them!"

Because women have been outside the ecclesiastical system for so long, many of them have less invested in a particular tradition or way of doing things and are more willing to try something new. "I think that it is the innovative and gutsy women in the clergy who are spearheading renewal in the church today," said Sam Gillespie, a layman in Washington, D.C., who stated that he had found the church to be "stale, unloving, bureaucratic, and as devoid of the Holy Spirit as a concrete block" until he got involved in a liturgical community led by a woman priest.

Women priests have brought a new sense of drama to the liturgy. The counterpoint of male and female voices from the altar, the variation in styles of gesture and accent, and the distinctive ways in which both men and women wear the same liturgical vestments bring to the worship service a symbolic sense of inclusiveness and unity that is absent when the sanctuary is the exclusive domain of men. Liturgy becomes "the work of the people" when all the people are represented.

The theological reality that the presence of women at the altar symbolizes, is the wholeness of God's creation—a God who is "neither male nor female," a God whose redeeming love is available equally to women and men, is simply more accessible to people who see that God represented by both women and men. "The ordination of women amazingly enhances the imaging of God's presence among us," declared Thomas Ray, bishop of Northern Michigan.

179

Again and again, parishioners have testified to that reality. "Knowing some clergywomen has reinforced for me the fact that God created male and female to be partners equally—not one subservient to the other," said a laywomen from Wyoming. "I feel that women have the ability to bring out the lovingness and motherliness of God, and I think we really need to know this side of God."

"My own understanding of priesthood has been challenged and strengthened by the presence of women," said Stephen J. White, rector of the Church of the Epiphany in the Diocese of Dallas. "Ordained women allow us to live the faith with integrity and prevent us from slipping back into the tired, old traditions of male oriented and dominated perceptions of the faith. Because of the ordination of women, I believe that we are more faithful in our understanding of the work and presence and very nature of God.